The Untold Story of Adele aus der Ohe

The Untold Story of *Adele aus der Ohe*

From a Liszt Student to a Virtuoso

LaWayne Leno

BEAVER'S POND
PRESS

ISBN: 978-1-59298-464-0

Library of Congress Control Number: 2012903008
Cover photo: MS Mus 132 (9), Houghton Library. Harvard University.
Book design by Ryan Scheife, Mayfly Design
Typeset in Filosofia

Printed in the United States of America
First Printing: 2012

16   15   14   13   12   5   4   3   2   1

Beaver's Pond Press, Inc.
7108 Ohms Lane, Edina, MN 55439-2129
(952) 829-8818 · www.BeaversPondPress.com

To order, visit www.BeaversPondBooks.com
or call (800) 901-3480. Reseller discounts available.

In fond remembrance of my piano teachers,
Belle Mehus and Alma Mehus-Studness

If God has given a gift there is also a place for it in this world.

~ Adele aus der Ohe

Contents

Acknowledgments   *xi*

Introduction   *xv*

Prelude   *xix*

1. Kullak and Liszt   *1*
2. America   *29*
3. Mr. and Mrs. Gilder   *45*
4. Tchaikovsky and Carnegie Hall   *75*
5. Travels   *99*
6. The Music   *111*
7. Mathilde   *151*
8. Berlin   *191*
9. Rachmaninoff   *231*

Postlude   *243*

Appendix A: Adele aus der Ohe's
   Published Compositions   *249*

Appendix B: Adele aus der Ohe's
   Concert Repertoire   *253*

Endnotes   *261*

Bibliography   *275*

About the Author   *281*

Acknowledgments

How does one adequately thank those who have enabled the realization of a near-lifelong dream? I only proceed, knowing full well that my words fall woefully short of expressing the gratitude my heart feels.

For those who provided information in the book's early stages—Jim Reske with his train expertise; Ron Stow from Stillwater, Minnesota, who provided early German translations; and the Kixmoeller family, Ken, Kim, Katie, and Susie, who spent an afternoon of their vacation at the Chicago Public Library on my behalf—I thank you all.

I had wonderfully helpful experiences with every library I contacted; without exception, the librarians I have worked with were professional, knowledgeable, and polite. Kevin Wilks at the Center for Research Libraries in Chicago, Peter Sewell at the Lily Library in Indiana, Sigrid Krause and Dr. Roland Schmidt-Hensel at the Berlin State Library, Evelyn Liepsch at the Goethe und Schiller Archive in Weimar, Joy Austria at the Newberry Library in Chicago, Rachel Howarth at the Houghton Library at Harvard, Charlotte Kolczynski at the Boston Public Library, Heidi Abbey and Martha Sachs at Penn State in Harrisburg, the staff at the New York Public Library and the Bavarian State Library in Munich, the staff at the Library of Congress in Washington, D.C., and at the Morgan Library and Museum in New York City, the libraries of Columbia University, Princeton University, Yale University, University of New Hampshire, University of Minnesota, and of course the very patient staff of my hometown library in White Bear Lake, Minnesota—I thank you all. You are all overworked and underpaid, your institutions are underfunded, and yet you do an admirable job!

To Brett Langston at the Tchaikovsky Research Project who provided the original Russian program for the final concert of Tchaikovsky's life, I am deeply indebted. He didn't know me, and knew nothing of my project, yet he willingly shared this program with me simply from an email request. Brett, I appreciate your kindness.

Birgit Klein of the Evangelical Lutheran Stadtkirchenverband in Hanover is fantastic. She researched the Ohe family records and provided me with the correct birthdates and names of the entire Ohe family. Without this data, my book would be woefully incomplete and I am ever so grateful for your patient and detailed work.

David Cannata and Rena Charnin Mueller are two resourceful New York professors who provided invaluable material and I thank you both.

Dennis James Bartel graciously allowed me to include his entertaining article about Tchaikovsky's time in Baltimore. It enriches the story and I am grateful for this generosity.

I want to posthumously thank Samuel Asbury of Texas for his work, which proved so very helpful to me. I know little of Mr. Asbury, except that he must have been a great fan of Miss aus der Ohe. In 1951 he compiled a paper that was an overview of aus der Ohe's career in Boston. His work was never published; Mr. Asbury simply had two copies hand-typed and bound, and donated one to the New York Public Library and one to the Harvard Library. With a modesty not unlike that of Miss aus der Ohe, he tells us nothing about himself in this compilation. He focuses exclusively on his subject. My sorriest regret for him is that he never knew the poem that closes this book, Richard Gilder's "Music in Darkness."

Anne-Marit Bergstrom is an angel disguised as a human! She is the most supportive and enthusiastic person I have ever met. She is the daughter of Alma Mehus-Studness, who had such a great reverence and love for her teacher, Adele aus der Ohe. Anne-Marit shared many wonderful documents and memories with me and constantly urged my project forward. Thank you so, so much!

And then there are my German translators, Brian and his wife Anja Buuck. How can I thank you? You did more for this book than I ever would have thought possible. Brian is brilliant, well educated, scholarly, hardworking, meticulous, and also a very nice person. Thank you, thank you, thank you!

And lastly, thanks to my partner and friend, Reid Smith, for his never-ending patience and passion for this project.

Introduction

The year 2011 was the bicentennial anniversary of the birth of the great piano virtuoso, Franz Liszt. Adele aus der Ohe, in her day, was one of Liszt's most celebrated students, so it seemed fitting to publish her first-ever biography as a birthday tribute to her great teacher. Imagine the surprise in discovering that 2011 was a milestone year for Adele aus der Ohe as well. Her family records from the churches of Hanover, Germany, prove that all birthdates attributed to her are in error and she was in fact born in 1861, 150 years ago.

Adele aus der Ohe was born and raised in Germany. She played her orchestral debut at the age of ten and became a student of Franz Liszt at the age of twelve, but her story is essentially an American story. She arrived in America young and unknown, was an immediate success, and quickly became one of the most sought-after artists of her day. She made her fame and fortune in America and was one of America's first musical superstars.

She toured from St. Petersburg, Russia, to San Francisco, California. She was a favorite of the Boston Symphony
and performed with this venerable organization an astonishing fifty-one times. When Carnegie Hall was dedicated,
the finest musicians of the day were engaged—Tchaikovsky
to conduct and aus der Ohe to solo. She became a friend of
Tchaikovsky and he invited her to St. Petersburg to perform
his Piano Concerto in B-flat minor at the same concert that
featured the premiere of his *Pathetique* Symphony, which
sadly turned out to be Tchaikovsky's final performance.
When renowned conductor Theodore Thomas was invited
"out West" to establish the Chicago Symphony, he engaged
aus der Ohe for the opening season. When the Minneapolis
Symphony was founded, aus der Ohe was asked to perform
her signature concerto, the Liszt E-flat, in the opening
season. When the Schubert Club of St. Paul, Minnesota,
inaugurated their International Artists Series they selected
aus der Ohe for the opening concert, demonstrating to the
world that they intended to present only the finest.

She was also a composer and her works were published
by G. Schirmer in New York and Ries & Erler in Germany.
She was a friend and champion of many of the leading
composers of her day, such as Amy Beach, Edward MacDowell, Arthur Foote, Henry Holden Huss, and Max Vogrich.

In her later years she lived and taught in Berlin, and late
in her life she befriended Sergei Rachmaninoff through an
exchange of lovely letters. She died in 1937, having survived
the First World War and the Great Inflation that followed.

In writing this first-ever biography of Adele aus
der Ohe, I strove to incorporate writings of the day. The

newspaper and magazine articles, letters, poetry, and various other commentary of the late nineteenth and early twentieth century give a wonderful sense of an age of sophistication and elegance that is long gone.

Adele was very much a woman of her time: a woman of refinement and dignity; a woman of principles and courage, of exquisite manners and politeness; and an astonishingly successful concert pianist.

ADELE AUS DER OHE AND FRANZ LISZT

The above, a rather poor-quality magazine clipping, is the
only copy of this photograph we have. The original was,
understandably, a prized possession of Miss aus der Ohe's.
She mailed it from Germany to America in 1899 so that it
could be reproduced as part of an article that appeared in
the *Criterion* magazine. It was subsequently returned to her
and has, like all of the personal possessions of Adele aus
der Ohe, vanished completely.

The original photo survived a journey across the ocean
but not a journey across time; we are left with this grainy,
yet still very precious, reproduction.

Prelude

by Albert Morris Bagby, *The Century Illustrated Monthly Magazine*, March 1888[1]

One sultry noonday in July 1885, a small group of musical celebrities from Berlin stood hatless—having converted their head coverings into temporary fans—in the shade of a low, uneven row of ancient houses in the city of Weimar, and expectantly watched the nearest turn in the street. Just as the heat was pronounced insupportable, two well-known figures sauntered arm in arm around the corner—one, the venerable form of Franz Liszt, his flowing white locks surmounted by an old-fashioned tile hat, his shirt-collar thrown open, revealing a throat which rivaled in color the high flush of his visage; and the other, Eugene d'Albert, a short youth with a round face and small black eyes, whose heavy shock of dark-brown hair fell about his neck à la Liszt and was topped by an artist's wide-brimmed slouch hat, the crown of which just brushed the master's shoulder.

It was not the odd contrasting couple that so forcibly impressed all beholders alike. It was the two great men of genius walking side by side—a tottering old man with one foot already in the grave, and his pupil, the younger by half a century and in the very springtime of life: one, the greatest piano virtuoso of any time, behind whom lay an unprecedentedly brilliant career of more than three-score years; the other, though scarcely more than a lad, the most famous musical artist of his generation, with a future of unlimited possibilities just opening up for him. Little d'Albert had only three years previously severed his lead- ing strings, and now with half of Europe at his feet, the central figure in the musical world that his genius had conquered, he returned to the guide and counselor of his student days. These two exchanged greetings with the gentlemen who had come, with d'Albert, on a twenty-four-hour visit to the city, and they crossed the stony way in a body to the cooler shade of Chemni- tiuss' restaurant garden to partake of a dinner in Liszt's honor.

This noteworthy meeting of master and pupil always recurs to my mind when asked, "Do any of Liszt's later pupils give promise of greatness, or at least of proving themselves emi- nently worthy of such a teacher?" If in reply I begin with Eugene d'Albert, it is because he was the first of the group to come prom- inently before the public; and justice to others compels me to add in the same sentence Arthur Friedheim, Alfred Reisenauer, Alexander Siloti, and Adele aus der Ohe.

It is easy to begin but more difficult to end the list, for I might add those fine artists who came already formed, later than the first five, to the master: Moriz Rosenthal, Conrad Ansorge, Bern- hard Stavenhagen . . . but the line must be drawn somewhere, though history will extend it.

Courtesy of Anne-Marit Bergstrom, Devil's Lake, North Dakota

Kullak and Liszt

Adelheit Johanne Auguste Hermine aus der Ohe[2] entered this world at 12:30 on the afternoon of February 11, 1861,[3] in Hanover, Germany. She began her life in the very same year the great piano virtuoso, Franz Liszt, who was to have such a profound impact on her, arrived at the half-century point in his life. She was the daughter of Johann Herrmann and Auguste Sophie Charlotte aus der Ohe.[4] Adelheit (Adele) was a treasured family name; it was the name of her grandmother, of several aunts, and one of the christening names given to her older sister, Luise Fernande.

Her father, Johann aus der Ohe, was originally from Badbergen in the Osnabrück district—an area west of Hanover—and was born in 1806. Her mother, born Auguste Bente in 1817, was from Hanover. At the time of their marriage in 1846, Johann aus der Ohe was already forty years old and Auguste was twenty-nine. They had four children: Sophie Adelheid[5] Louise Ferdinandine (born December 11, 1848), Bernhardine Mathilde Henriette (born September 7, 1850), Ferdinand Carl Hermann Gustav (born October 15, 1852), and finally Adele in 1861. At the time of Adele's birth her father was fifty-five years old and her mother was forty-four. Her oldest sister, Luise Fernande, was already thirteen, her sister Mathilde was eleven, and her brother Gustav was nine.

Dr. aus der Ohe had a Ph.D. in philology (the study of languages in historical writings) and held several teaching positions during his career. At the time of Mathilde and Gustav's births he was a language teacher at Quakenbrück, a town quite near to where he was born. The family subsequently moved to Hanover where, at the time of Adele's birth, he was a professor at the Lyceum.

Adele exhibited extraordinary musical ability at a very early age. Her parents discovered that she had the gift of perfect pitch, the ability to accurately identify musical tones. "She could tell the notes that were struck on the piano, without seeing them, before she could pronounce their names. The baby girl found it hard to say 'Fis' (F) and 'Gis' (G), but she could go to the keyboard and point out the keys that had been touched."[6] Johann and Auguste quickly realized that the musical opportunities available in Hanover were inadequate for someone as talented as their daughter. Berlin was one of the great musical cities of Europe and many of the finest teachers and performers of the day were located there. The family decided it was the best place for Adele's musical instruction. Dr. aus der Ohe obtained a teaching position in Berlin and in December of 1869, when Adele was eight years old, he was able to relocate his family to the German capital.

Upon their arrival in Berlin, Adele enrolled in Theodor Kullak's *Neue Akademie der Tonkunst* (New Academy of

Musical Art). Theodor Kullak was one of the most esteemed piano teachers of the nineteenth century. He was born in 1818, nine years prior to Beethoven's death, and had himself been a student of that most famous of all of Beethoven's students and friends, Carl Czerny. In 1851, Kullak established his *Neue Akademie der Tonkunst* in Berlin, specializing in the training of pianists. It became the largest private music school in Germany. By the time aus der Ohe enrolled in 1870, the school boasted a hundred teachers and eleven hundred students. Dr. Kullak himself undertook the training of Adele aus der Ohe.

Her progress was astonishing and by 1872, at the mere age of ten, Adele played Beethoven's Piano Concerto No. 2 in B-flat at her orchestral debut in Berlin. Amy Fay was in the audience.

Amy Fay was a young and talented American who went to Europe in the 1870s to further her piano studies. She was at the forefront of that wave of Americans who flocked to Europe over the course of the next half-century in order to obtain the European credentials that were a prerequisite for American success. She wrote frequent letters to her family back in America, which were subsequently compiled in her book, *Music-Study in Germany in the Nineteenth Century*. These letters are famous for their witty and entertaining observations, as well as for their value as insightful sources of information.

In May of 1872, in one of these wonderful letters, Amy Fay wrote, "He [Kullak] has one little fairy of a scholar ten years old. Her name is Adele aus der Ohe—(isn't that an old knightly name?)—and it is the most astonishing thing to hear that child play! I heard her play a concerto of Beethoven's the other day with orchestral accompaniment and a great cadenza by Moscheles absolutely perfectly. She never missed a note all the way through."[7]

Later, in December of that same year (1872), Dr. Kullak referred to this Beethoven performance in a certificate[8] he issued on Adele's behalf.

Zeugniß
der
Neuen Academie der Tonkunst.

Adele aus der Ohe hat auch im verflossenen Jahre ihre ausgezeichneten musikalischen Anlagen in erfreulichster Weise weiter entwickelt. Sie hat u[nter] A[nderem] bei Gelegenheit der Osterprüfung im Saale der Singakademie ein Konzert von Beethoven in so correkter und kunstverständiger Weise vorgetragen, daß ihr reichster und wohlverdienter Beifall zu Theil wurde.

Es ist für mich kein Zweifel, daß sie, wenn sie in stetiger Weise weiter schreitet eine sehr bedeutende Künstlerin werden wird. Sie ist daher jeder ihr etwa zu Theil werdenden Unterstützung vollkommen würdig.

Berlin den 25ten Dezember 1872.

Professor Dr. Th[eodor] Kullak, königlicher Hofpianist und Hofpianist S[einer] kaiserl[ichen] und königl[ichen] Hoheit des Kronprinzen, Director der neuen Akademie der Tonkunst

---

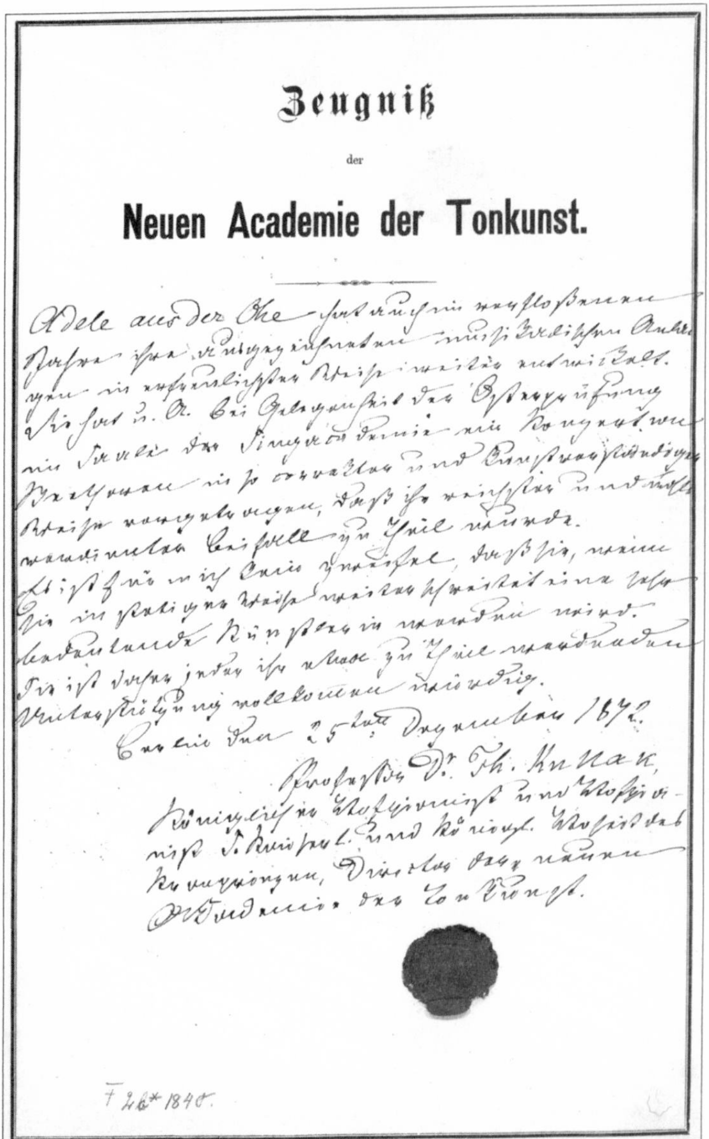
Zeugniß
der
Neuen Academie der Tonkunst.
Adele aus der Ohe

bpk, Berlin/Staatsbibliothek zu Berlin/Art Resource, NY

**Certificate
of the
New Academy of Musical Art**

*Adele aus der Ohe has continued to develop her excel-
lent musical talents in the most delightful manner
in the past year as well. Among other things, she performed a concerto of Beethoven's in the auditorium of
the Voice Academy on the occasion of the Easter exam
in such a correct and artistic manner that she received
hearty and well-earned applause.*

*I have no doubt that she will become a distin-
guished artist if she continues to advance in a steady
manner. She is therefore worthy of any support that she
might receive.*

Berlin, December 25, 1872

*Professor Dr. Theodor Kullak, the royal court pia-
nist and the court pianist of His Imperial and Royal
Highness the Crown Prince, director of the New Academy of Musical Art.*

While this certificate is a lovely testament to her amazing abilities and a wonderful compliment, it most likely was
intended to serve a very specific and practical purpose—to
secure a patron!

Johann aus der Ohe was a professor at one of the prestigious military academies of Berlin. His teaching position

surely paid him a salary adequate to provide his family with a comfortable middle class lifestyle. A professor's salary, however, would not be adequate to provide the sort of education and opportunities that a talent such as his daughter's required. It was imperative to find, among the wealthy nobility, a patron. This was secured in Princess Alma of Carolath-Beuthin. With this patronage, aus der Ohe was set to spread her wings wide and soar as only she could.

It was inevitable that such a *Wunderkind* would find her way to the greatest living pianist and teacher of the day. And so she did, becoming Franz Liszt's student when she was barely in her teens. She continued to work with him for the rest of his life.

We do not know exactly when or where aus der Ohe first met Liszt, but most of the contemporary biographical data indicates that she was twelve when she began to study with him, which would have been in 1873. Her family might have been preparing for these lessons for some time. Possibly, following her spring orchestral debut in 1872, her father requested an endorsement from Kullak, which Kullak provided in the form of the certificate he issued in December. Her father then used this endorsement to solicit a patron who could provide the necessary funds, so that by the summer of 1873 everything was in order for aus der Ohe to travel to Weimar to begin her work with the great master himself. Liszt quickly developed a deep fondness for the talented young prodigy. It was reported, "when about thirteen years old, after having been with him only a year, she created a furor at one of Liszt's royal concerts, under the special patronage of the Grand Duke, who was astonished at what seemed to him her phenomenal talent."[9]

Carl Lachmund, like Amy Fay, was another American student in Germany. As a twenty-three-year-old, he heard an impromptu performance by Franz Liszt and became an immediate devotee. He eventually became a student of Liszt and during his studies kept detailed diaries, which were later published as a book entitled *Living With Liszt*. In his diaries, Lachmund reprinted a letter from his friend and fellow Liszt student, Constantin von Sternberg. In the letter, Sternberg recalled that in the autumn of 1875, he, Pohlig[10], and aus der Ohe followed Liszt to Rome to continue their studies over the winter after a summer in Weimar. Sternberg mentioned in the letter that he failed to meet Adele aus der Ohe in Rome, "although I knew that she, too, was a frequent visitor at the Villa d'Este."[11]

Aus der Ohe's performances in Weimar in 1877 were included by *The Musical World* among the highlights of that year: "During the summer season just passed, the Abbate Franz Liszt gave twelve Musical Matinees at his residence...the more important compositions included: *Geisterschiff*[12] by Tausig (Mlle. aus der Ohe) and the Funeral March from *Götterdämmerung*, eight-handed pianoforte arrangement by Rupp (the Abbate Franz Liszt, Herren Pohlig, Coonen,[13] and Mlle. aus der Ohe)."[14] She was sixteen that summer and performing eight-hand repertoire with Liszt himself taking one of the parts—quite an accomplishment. A concert program that included an eight-hand piano arrangement of opera music may seem quite unusual to us now, but one must remember the context of this performance. These were pre-recording days and it was not unusual to play piano arrangements of orchestral pieces in order to give listeners a chance to hear this music. Liszt had transcribed all nine symphonies of Beethoven just for this purpose. Also Wagner's epic Ring Cycle, of which *Götterdämmerung* is the final opera, had received its premiere only one year earlier, in August of 1876. This music would have been unfamiliar to most people, and quite likely Liszt wished to make it better known.

Aus der Ohe performed frequently throughout Germany during her teenage years and in 1879 she wrote to her great teacher, apparently seeking some sort of assistance concerning one of her concert tours. Neither aus der Ohe's original letter nor Liszt's response has survived. We do, however, have a fascinating draft[15] of the letter Liszt wrote to aus der Ohe. It is a wonderful insight into the meticulous care Liszt took in writing his letters.

Foto: Klassik Stiftung Weimar

---

5 Sept[ember] [18]79–Roma

Adele aus der Ohe

Sehr geehrtes Fräulein,

Auf Concert Tournéen habe ich nicht den gerings-
ten Einfluss. Indess[en]...Wenn Sie meiner hohen
Kunstgenossin Frau Jachmann-Wagner ~~sagen wollen,~~
~~dass ich Sie beständig hoch verehre, was~~ *sagen wol-*
len, dass ihrer Gewogenheit die vortreffliche Pianistin
Adele aus der Ohe besonders empfiehlt, ist damit ganz
einverstanden.

Freundlichst ergeben
Fr[anz] Liszt

Aufrichtigen Dank für die Zeilen ihres / für die freund-
lichen Zeilen ihres Herrn Vaters
   Für die freundlichen Zeilen ihres Herrn Vaters
danke ich aufrichtig.

September 5, 1879— Rome

Adele aus der Ohe
Honorable Mademoiselle,
I do not have the slightest influence on concert tours.
In this . . .
   If you want to tell my great artistic colleague Mrs.
Jachmann-Wagner that I constantly hold you in high
regard, which that the accomplished pianist Adele aus
der Ohe is especially recommended to her favor, is com-
pletely in agreement with that.

In friendship
Franz Liszt

Sincere thanks for the words your / for the kind words
written by your esteemed father
   For the kind words written by your esteemed father
I offer my sincere thanks.[16]

It is interesting to try to "read" the emotions and intent (between the lines, so to speak) as well as the content of this draft. Liszt began the note with a rather sternly emphatic statement that he has no influence on concert tours, almost as if he is annoyed at the request. Yet, ever eager to provide any assistance he could to his students, he immediately softened and gave his complete endorsement, just in case he actually did have some influence on concert tours. Especially interesting is how carefully Liszt chose his words. For whatever reason, he crossed out the phrase, "That I constantly hold you in high regard." One can almost sense the spontaneity of this comment, and then upon further reflection, his realization that perhaps this phrase, while a sincere expression of his feelings, was not the best phrase for the purposes of this letter. Liszt is so meticulous that he even took three revisions to find exactly the phrase he wanted when offering his thanks to her father. What an interesting glimpse into the old master's great and exacting mind!

In either 1880 or 1881, Adele's father died. Johann aus der Ohe was about seventy-five years old at the time of his death and was most likely retired from his teaching career; however, his death would still have been a great loss to the family, financially as well as emotionally. Any retirement pension he might have been receiving would have ceased. Additionally around this time, her patroness, Princess Alma, died. So aus der Ohe, now just barely out of her teenage years, had to rely on her own resources—concert revenues plus whatever her mother, brother, and two sisters could manage to spare on her behalf for her livelihood and studies.

While Liszt never accepted any payment for his lessons, to study with Liszt was nevertheless a rather expensive undertaking. One had to travel to wherever Liszt happened to be at the time, usually Weimar in the summer and Rome in the winter, and once there it was necessary to obtain lodging, food, and of course, a piano for practicing. Concert income was a necessity in order for her piano instruction to continue.

By 1883 aus der Ohe was already meriting the sort of accolades she was to earn for the rest of her career. A foreign correspondent for the British publication *The Monthly Musical Record* wrote in February 1883, "...the pleasure... in hearing one of our 'native' pianists, Fräulein Adele aus der Ohe, at the last Monday concert. This young artist, a pupil of the late Theodor Kullak, and known to the Berlin public for several years as a talent *'hors ligne'* [in a class by herself], has attained an unusual degree of perfection since she undertook last summer the pilgrimage to Weimar, necessary to every worshipper of the piano, and studied during several months with Franz Liszt...I am willing to subscribe to the judgment of our most competent critics, who declare Frl. aus der Ohe equal to her great rivals, Sophie Menter and Annette Essipov."[17]

In this same article the author provided a sense of the stir aus der Ohe created at Weimar: "As I know by confidential communication, there was not one among the great number of young artists, either male or female, who met for the same purpose last summer in Weimar, with the exception of d'Albert, who excited the interest of the 'Gross-Meister' to the same degree as Adele aus der Ohe."

Photo by Louis Held, Weimar 1883. Courtesy of David Cannata and Rena Charnin Mueller

We owe many valuable photos of Liszt and his pupils to the photographer Louis Held, who arrived in Weimar in 1882. It became customary to take a group picture each year and this is the photo of the 1883 class. The three women seated on the far left are Adele aus der Ohe, her mother Augusta, and her sister Mathilde. The man standing just above and to the right of Mathilde is Alexander Siloti. Alfred Reisenauer is in the center, wearing the light tan suit and with his hands in his pockets. Carl Lachmund is to the right, standing with one foot on the steps, and his wife is the lady in a black dress standing between the two women in white dresses. Liszt is at the upper right window and his servant is the figure in the upper left window. The building is the Hofgärtnerei. The Grand Duke of Weimar owned this home and made it available to Liszt during his annual stays in Weimar. It was in the upper floor studio, the room in which Liszt is standing as he peers out the window, that the famous master lessons occurred.

———————

Carl Lachmund recalled a June 1883 master class: "Adele aus der Ohe had a considerable future behind her in her juvenile years...the *Fräulein* played Schumann's *Carnaval* with beautiful touch and tonal modulations, ease, and assurance..."[18]

The *Monthly Musical Record* reiterated praise when noting of a fall 1883 Berlin recital: "...the piano recital of Adele aus der Ohe, a pupil of Kullak's Conservatory, who showed in Bach's *Italian* Concerto, in Schumann's *Carnaval*, and in smaller pieces by Silas, Moszkowski, Liszt, and Tausig, the astonishing progress she has made under the direction of Liszt during her last stay in Weimar..."[19]

Carl Lachmund departed Weimar just as the Austrian pianist August Göllerich was arriving. Lachmund began his third year of study with Liszt in May of 1884 and stayed until he bid his final farewell to Liszt in July. Göllerich, on the other hand, had just arrived in Weimar in May of 1884 and on May 31 attended his first class. He too, like Lachmund, kept diaries, which were also later published as a book entitled *The Piano Master Classes of Franz Liszt 1884–1886*. These two diarists, Lachmund and Göllerich, thus provide a seamless documentation of the teaching of Franz Liszt during the final years of his life. Göllerich did not record any performances by aus der Ohe in 1884.

It was for a very sad reason that Adele did not attend Liszt's 1884 classes: her mother died. Auguste aus der Ohe was sixty-seven years old at the time of her death. The older children were already well into adulthood—Luise Fernande, Mathilde, and Gustav were all in their thirties by then. Adele, on the other hand, being so much younger than her siblings, was still very much a young lady, only in her very early twenties, and the loss of her mother was felt deeply.

Adele found herself bereft of parental guidance and affection and she turned to her siblings to fill the void. She and her sisters formed an impenetrable bond and the three of them remained very close their entire lives. None of the Ohe siblings ever married or had children. They were a solid family block and allowed for no intrusions. Luise Fernande and Gustav lived in Berlin in the family home while Mathilde accompanied Adele as she traveled the world. Every year Mathilde and Adele returned to Berlin and the four siblings were reunited, even if sometimes for only a short while in the summer.

Quite possibly the deaths of her parents so early in her life deepened many of the qualities that were already so marked in aus der Ohe: serious, hardworking, conscientious, a strong sense of duty, and an amazing stoicism when confronted with adversity.

Aus der Ohe resumed her studies with Liszt in Weimar in the summer of 1885. It was also in 1885 that she first met Albert Morris Bagby, whose kindness and generosity proved to be so important so many years into the future, during the final years of her life.

Albert Bagby, like Amy Fay, Carl Lachmund, and so many others, was another young American who made his way to Europe to study with Liszt. He and aus der Ohe both attended Liszt's 1885 classes at Weimar and during these student days developed the friendship that lasted the rest of their lives.

Albert Bagby later became a highly respected figure in the New York musical scene. For fifty years, he managed his "Musical Mornings" in the ballroom of the Waldorf Astoria. Eight times each season at 11:00 A.M., the fashionable

ADELE, HER MOTHER AUGUSTA, AND HER SISTER MATHILDE AUS DER OHE. (NOTE
THE STRIKING RESEMBLANCE OF ADELE TO HER MOTHER)
(An enlargement from Louis Held's 1883 photo outside the Hofgärtnerei.)

elite gathered to hear some of the greatest musical artists.
He frequently invited aus der Ohe to perform at these
musicales.

It was Mr. Bagby who wrote an eloquent and informa-
tive introduction of aus der Ohe to the American public
for *The Century Illustrated Monthly Magazine*.[20] *The Century*
was one of the most popular and widely read magazines
in America and was a forerunner to similarly successful
magazines such as *The Saturday Evening Post*, *Life*, and *Time*.

When Mr. Bagby's article was published in March 1888, aus der Ohe was already a brilliant success in America and there was great curiosity about her background.

At a large musicale in Berlin one evening in February, 1885, I first met Adele aus der Ohe. Upon reminding her that I had made her acquaintance in America several years previously, she exclaimed in surprise, "How is that possible? I have never been there."

"Through Miss Fay's book," I replied.

"Ah!" she said, and smiled. "Then you made my acquaintance at an early age. I hope though to go to America some day."

That wish was to be fulfilled earlier than she then thought. Unheralded and comparatively unknown, Fräulein aus der Ohe landed in New York in October 1886. Her brilliant success in the metropolis and the principal cities of the Union is too recent to need recapitulation.

Aus der Ohe is the name of a very old and noble German family, dating from the eleventh or twelfth century, when various prefixes—i.e. van, au, zu, aus, etc.—denoted high birth. Many families afterward altered the original form to the more common von; but the Ohes have retained the ancient aus before their patronymic. The pianist is a daughter of the late Professor aus der Ohe, of the Royal Artillery and Engineers' School at Berlin, but formerly of Hanover, where she was born and passed the first five or six years of her life.

When three-and-a-half years old she first gave evidence of her remarkable talent. An elder sister was strumming Arditi's "Il bacio" one day in the nursery where the children were at play. When she had finished, the tiny Adele, crying, "Ich! Ich!," begged to be placed on the stool, and to their astonishment repeated the entire waltz, giving the correct bass with her left hand.

"Mamma! Papa!" cried the children in chorus as they threw open the door: "Come! Come and hear Adelchen!" There was great rejoicing that day in the family Ohe. The parents themselves began at once to instruct her in piano playing.

In her fifth year she became acquainted with the talented musical couple Bronsart,[21] who took her to Hans von Bülow[22] for advice. "Let me first look in her eyes," he said, and continued, "Yes, there really is music there!"

He proposed that she be placed under his instruction at Munich where he was then residing, but the fond parents could not consent to a separation from so young a child. Adele was seven years old[23] when Professor aus der Ohe moved with his family to Berlin. Here she became a pupil of Franz Kullak, and several months later of his father, the celebrated Dr. Theodor Kullak, with whom she remained until her thirteenth year.

At eight years of age she made her first public appearance. Two years later she gave concerts with orchestra at Berlin and Hanover in which she played Beethoven's B-flat major Concerto with the Moscheles Cadenza.

Shortly after leaving Kullak she came to Liszt at Weimar and, barring occasional interruptions, benefited by seven years of his instruction. Several long concert tours—the first when in her fourteenth year—were made during this period in Germany. Previous to her American debut she had never played outside her native land. At her last public appearance there she performed Taubert's Piano Concerto in the four hundredth Jubilee Soiree of the Royal Orchestra, with that superb body of musicians, at the Berlin Royal Opera House.

In the salons of the German capital Adele aus der Ohe is as great a social as musical favorite. She enjoyed the friendship and chaperonage of the late lamented Princess Alma of Carolath-Beuthin, a noble woman, distinguished for her charities and as a patroness of the fine arts. She is very popular at the Imperial Palace, where she has often played privately and in state concerts.

Adele aus der Ohe is not merely a gifted musical artiste, but a young woman of varied accomplishments. Besides her mother tongue, she speaks and writes French, Italian, and English; is a student in the arts and sciences; writes poetry, and is a composer of music—under an assumed name. She has been rightly taught to believe in the necessity of a broad and liberal education for all who aspire above mediocrity in her chosen profession.

After hearing her play and meeting her almost daily in Weimar, I comprehended Liszt's deferential bearing towards her, which had struck me the first time

*I saw her at his lessons. As he honored the true gen-
tlewoman, just so did he admire her intellectual and
artistic gifts. Although Liszt was ever willing and ready
to aid young pianists from the wealth of his knowledge,
he was exceedingly discriminating and gave in plenty
only to those who evinced uncommon aptitude. The
earnestness of his work with Adele aus der Ohe was
the most telling compliment he could pay the mental
endowments of any pupil.*

*She was by all odds the best among the ladies,
and one of the most accomplished artists in his class.
He habitually commented upon her improvisations
introductory to a piano composition, and frequently
bade her extricate some frightened player from the
dangers of an impromptu prelude. At his especial
request she compiled a volume of such preludes and
modulations, which he desired her to dedicate to him.
This Fräulein aus der Ohe did—though it has not yet
been published—and sent Liszt a copy of the same. It
gave him much pleasure, as I can substantiate.*[24]

*In the lessons he frequently remarked her "intre-
pidity" and "fearless certainty" in playing; and in
one of the last soirees musicales that he gave, said in
an aside, "She has a wonderful touch; it is like velvet!"
Perhaps I heard him express himself more in approval
of Adele aus der Ohe's performances than of any others;
for she had been absent from Weimar some time when
she returned in 1885, and her splendid artistic development was a source of gratification to him. In his letters*

*to her, Liszt varied the conventional form of address to
"My honored colleague," "My dear virtuoso," etc.*

*Her public life is so arduous that Fräulein aus der
Ohe finds little time for society. Her personal tastes are
quiet and unassuming. Once I heard her retort rather
warmly to a complimentary remark of a friend, "I have
no time to be vain or conceited. My art is holy to me
and requires my every effort. If there is anything that I
dislike, it is an arrogant artist. He should be thankful
to God that He has given him such talent, and guard it
sacredly." Such sentiments add dignity to the character
of a great artist like Adele aus der Ohe.*

August Göllerich documented frequent performances
by aus der Ohe over the course of Liszt's 1885 Weimar classes. Already at the very first class, on June 16, aus der Ohe
played a Zarebski polonaise, and Göllerich remembered,
"the lady played a very interesting prelude that pleased
the master very much."[25] At the third lesson, on June 20,
aus der Ohe played another polonaise of Zarebski's, and
on June 22, she played one of Robert Schumann's greatest
masterpieces, the Fantasy in C major, which Schumann
had dedicated to Liszt.

Liszt was very pleased with aus der Ohe's performance,
saying, "That is a very beautiful piece! The first theme
very powerful and audacious."[26] Göllerich noted that at
particular phrases Liszt said, "not at all conservatoryish."
(From Liszt this was high praise; he hated the music conservatories of the day.) Liszt was completely transported
by the ending of the first movement and said, "That is

wonderfully refined and noble." She must have played the Schumann Fantasy especially well, for this piece became a permanent part of her repertoire and she often performed it in concert throughout the rest of her life.

At the fifth class on June 27, aus der Ohe played three of Liszt's *Transcendental Etudes*: *Eroica*, *Ricordanza*, and the F minor.

The following day she performed Liszt's Second *Mephisto Waltz* at what must have been one of the more unusual, yet probably very delightful, social events in Weimar: a Sunday afternoon soiree at the Stahr sisters' residence.

The Stahr sisters, Anna and Helena, were eccentric spinsters who were lifelong residents of Weimar and they absolutely idolized Liszt. They always dressed alike, and always in the fashion of about thirty years earlier when they were young women—looking like two "school girls at a Sunday school picnic." They flitted around with great energy, dispensing *Kaffee* und *Kaffeekuchen* (coffee served in dainty china cups and home-baked German coffeecake), and chatted with everyone. One observer described them as characters right out of a Charles Dickens novel. They had had lessons with Liszt in his early years at Weimar and kept one room in their home entirely filled with Liszt memorabilia of every kind. They regularly opened their home to his students, the "Lisztianer," for Sunday afternoon musical performances, and it was said that you really had not "been" to Weimar until you attended one of the Stahr sisters' Sunday Afternoons. Liszt had known them for many years, liked them very much, and was a frequent guest.

At the June 29 class, aus der Ohe played Liszt's *Lie-bestraum* No. 3 and Liszt commented, "You must play this frivolous somewhat songlike piece exactly like that."[27]

The Göllerich diaries give a sense of the large amount of repertoire she had "in her fingers" and the unusual frequency of her performances for Liszt. At the August 14 class she played Liszt's Hungarian Rhapsody No. 9. On August 16 she played the Auber-Liszt *Tarantella di Bravura*, and the following day, Liszt's transcription of Wagner's *Liebestod*. On August 19 she played Liszt's transcription of Bach's Fantasy and Fugue in G minor and the Strauss-Tausig *Nachtfalter* (Moths), and on August 23 Liszt's Third *Mephisto Waltz*.

Liszt relocated to Rome for the winter and Göllerich noted that on December 3, aus der Ohe sight-read some preludes for Liszt. (Liszt considered sight-reading a valuable skill and we occasionally read of him requesting his students to sight-read.)

Franz Liszt was one of the greatest musical personalities ever to live and volumes have been written about him. Yet after 200 years, he still remains somewhat of an enigma. Liszt was one of the most successful concert pianists ever, yet he gave his final public performances when at the very height of his fame, in 1847, at the age of thirty-five. While he never married, he was the father of three children. In his early fifties, he received minor orders of ministry within the Catholic Church. He composed some of the greatest music of all time, yet also penned compositions that rate rather low in critical esteem. While a great respecter of the music of the past, transcribing Bach and urging the performance of Beethoven, he was also a great visionary. Throughout his entire life he was a champion of the music and musicians of the future, both composers and performers.

As a teacher, as in so many other things, Liszt was completely innovative. His teaching was like that of no other. He never gave private lessons and he taught no technique. He created the "Master Class" concept where everything is done before an audience. Liszt's master classes had very little structure. As the students arrived they placed their music scores on the piano, open to whatever piece they wished to play. The class began when Liszt entered the room. The students all stood and Liszt would slowly make his way to the front of the room, greeting various students as he passed by them. Liszt looked over the accumulated pile of music and, when he spotted something he wished to hear, he announced his choice and the hapless owner of the score would proceed to the piano. Liszt might say nothing, a few words, or a great deal. He might demonstrate or he might not. He might be kind and complimentary or he might deliver searing criticism—and the students flocked to him by the hundreds.

By May of 1886, Liszt was seventy-four years old and in very poor health. Aus der Ohe's final performance for her great teacher was in one of his last classes, on May 28, 1886. She played Zarebski's Grand Polonaise Op. 6 and Liszt's own *Mephisto Waltz* No. 2.

Liszt's daughter Cosima, who was the wife of Richard Wagner, invited Liszt to come to Bayreuth for the summer to attend the annual Bayreuth Festival performances of Wagner's operas. Many questioned the wisdom of Liszt traveling while in such poor health, and some also questioned the motives of Cosima's invitation, feeling that Cosima was more concerned with the income-generating possibilities of Liszt's presence in Bayreuth rather than her father's fragile health. Nevertheless, Liszt agreed to the trip. At the end of June, Liszt bade his students a tearful goodbye and departed Weimar for Bayreuth where, at 11:30 P.M., on July 31, 1886, the legendary Franz Liszt died.

Aus der Ohe's student days had come to an end—one incredible chapter in her life was now over, and another, even greater, was about to begin. She had been receiving instruction from Liszt as early as 1873. Of all the many, many Liszt students, aus der Ohe's association with the master was one of the longest, encompassing a period of more than ten years. What memories, inspiration, encouragement, thoughts, and emotions she must have carried in her heart and mind after all those years of study with one of the greatest pianists ever to live. Did ever a pianist go forth into the world with greater endorsement?

949 BROADWAY, N.Y.

Courtesy, The Lilly Library, Indiana University, Bloomington, Indiana

America

In the late fall of 1886, Adele aus der Ohe, accompanied by her sister Mathilde, arrived on the shores of America. She had been offered an invitation to perform in New York and she jumped at the opportunity. Possibly the invitation had been obtained with the help of one of the American students attending Liszt's final classes in Weimar, and quite possibly it was her good friend, Albert Bagby, who facilitated this opportunity. She had hoped to go to America and now it was happening. It must have been an incredibly exciting time in her life. She was twenty-five years old, exploring the world for the first time, and soon to make her American debut as a concert pianist.

The New York City that Adele and Mathilde arrived at in 1886 was every bit as dynamic and vibrant for the people of that time as it is for the people of our time, although it was decidedly different from the city we now know. With a population nearing 1.5 million people, it was the largest city in America. The automobile was still several decades into the future so transportation around the city was either by rail (trains and streetcars), horse and carriage, or foot. The city's first luxury apartment building, the Dakota, had opened only two years earlier, in 1884. It was located in the remote and sparsely inhabited Upper West side of Manhattan, way up on 72nd Street and surrounded by nothing but open space. Some said it was aptly named since it was as remote as the Dakota Territory!

Electric streetlights were the latest technological wonder and the world's largest bridge at the time of its construction, the Brooklyn Bridge, had opened only three years earlier, in 1883. It provided the first land passage between Manhattan and the still independent city of Brooklyn, New York.

As their ship steamed into New York Harbor, Adele and Mathilde were some of the first people to view the newly erected and already famous gift from France to the United States. The aus der Ohe sisters arrived literally within days of the dedication of the Statue of Liberty, which occurred on October 28, 1886.

The elegant Belvedere Hotel, at the corner of 4th Avenue and 18th Street, was conveniently located in the midst of the downtown area of Manhattan. It was aus der Ohe's favorite hotel and the one where she always stayed when in the city. All of the city's major concert halls were within walking distance of the Belvedere Hotel. One block away, at the corner of 5th Avenue and 18th Street, stood Chickering Hall. Built by

Chickering Hall

the Chickering Piano Company, it was one of the popular recital halls, and with a seating capacity of 1,450 it could accommodate orchestral or solo performances. A notable feature was a large organ installed on both sides of the stage.

A short distance away, at 73 East 14th Street, stood Steinway Hall. Built by Chickering's competitor, the Steinway Piano Company, it was one of the largest concert halls in the city. It could seat 2,500 people and was home to the New York Philharmonic for the first twenty-five years of the orchestra's existence.

Further uptown, on 40th Street just east of Broadway, was Mendelssohn Hall. It was home to the Mendelssohn Glee Club and, with a seating capacity of 1,100 people, was another popular recital hall. A striking feature of this hall was the huge twin panel murals on either side of the proscenium arch that had been commissioned specifically for the hall.

Finally, just a short walk from Mendelssohn Hall, on Broadway between 39th and 40th streets, stood the grand Metropolitan Opera House. It was the largest concert hall in New York in 1886 with seating for over 3,500 and was noted for its excellent acoustics and elegant interior.

Miss aus der Ohe appeared in all of these venues during her first seasons in America, but sadly none of them exist any longer. All of these concert halls, as well as her favorite Belvedere Hotel, have been demolished.

To fill these concert halls with great music, the city had three major orchestras, each with its own conductor, offering the New York public ample listening opportunities. The renowned Theodore Thomas was one of the first great conductors in America and was music director of the Philharmonic Society, known now as the New York Philharmonic, when aus der Ohe arrived in 1886. He, like aus der Ohe, was originally from Hanover, although his family had moved to America when he was ten years old. One can imagine the instant camaraderie that would have been established between these two fine musicians and native Hanoverians.

Walter Damrosch, also German-born, was conductor of the Symphony Society—a rival to the Philharmonic Society until the two orchestras merged in 1928. Having been born in 1862, he was only twenty-four, one year younger than aus der Ohe, when she first soloed under his baton. His father, Leopold Damrosch, had originally worked with Liszt and had been the concert master of Liszt's orchestra in Weimar. At the time of aus der Ohe's arrival in America, Leopold Damrosch had only recently died, in February of 1885, and his young son, Walter, had taken over his father's directorship of the Symphony Society.

The third in this triumvirate of New York conductors was Anton Seidl, conductor of the Metropolitan Opera. He was Hungarian by birth, German trained, and had worked closely with Richard Wagner at Bayreuth. He was a brilliant opera conductor and was highly praised by Wagner. He later succeeded Theodore Thomas as the head of the Philharmonic Society. It was at one of Mr. Seidl's concerts that aus der Ohe made her brilliant entrance into American musical history.

On December 23, 1886, an unknown pianist, Miss Adele aus der Ohe, walked onto the stage of Steinway Hall, accompanied by the great maestro, Anton Seidl. One can easily visualize the first few moments—Miss aus der Ohe settling on the bench, adjusting her dress, nodding to the conductor to indicate her readiness to begin. Mr. Seidl raising his baton, the opening theme of the Liszt Concerto in E-flat sounding in the orchestra, and suddenly those crashing octaves from the piano—and by the end of the performance, Adele aus der Ohe was famous:

> ...the end of the chosen work had not been reached before the listeners felt that a new power, a new gift and a fresh art were before them, while when the end did come, a great triumph came with it, and—as the phrase runs—came to stay. For wherever she has since appeared common enthusiasm has at once seized upon the critic and the layman, the audience, the conductor, and the accompanying orchestra. And the verdict of cool subsequent reflection has turned to sustain the impression first produced in the heat of surprise, delight, and enthusiasm.[28]

The newspapers were ecstatic. The *New York Times* reported the following day:

> ...a performance of Liszt's Piano Concerto No. 1 in E♭, which was not only interesting and in some respects striking, but which produced a pianist of remarkable powers and of still more notable promise...The pianist was quite unknown to an American audience, and her debut claims a few words of comment. Fräu-

lein aus der Ohe is one of the few pupils of Liszt that are really entitled to the distinction the name confers. It was once the habit of piano students who were presented to the master and permitted to play a few minutes in his presence to call themselves his pupils ever afterward; Fräulein aus der Ohe, luckily stands on a different footing and has bought the right to her title by protracted study under Liszt's guidance. We have many excellent pianists of the gentler sex in the United States, the list being headed by Mme. Essipov, who is still first and foremost among her contemporaries. Without reviving ancient memories or instituting comparisons, however, it may be said that nothing less than a virtuoso of extraordinary powers would be likely to astound such a metropolitan audience as was gathered at Steinway Hall last evening... In response to most enthusiastic recalls Fräulein aus der Ohe came forward after the concerto, and rendered with unflagging strength Liszt's Polonaise in E major. She is the stuff of which great artists are made though some years may be required to bring her excellence to ripeness...[29]

The *New York Mail and Express* announced, "Fräulein aus der Ohe... fairly took the audience by storm... a brilliant future may be predicted for this young pianist."[30]

The *New York World* wrote, "It must be admitted that in Frl. aus der Ohe, New York has at the present moment one of the most surprisingly talented and skillful pianists that has been heard here for years... she has immense strength; but her hand of iron, with fingers of steel, is incased in a velvet glove…"[31]

The *New York Evening Post*: "Her very first bars must have convinced the audience that she was what she claimed to be: a pupil of Liszt. Such brilliancy of execution, such verve and vigor of execution can only be learned by the contagious example of Liszt or Rubinstein…"[32]

The *New York Sun:* "…She plays as naturally as a bird flies, with a sort of willful freedom and healthy dash that are extremely fascinating…"[33]

The *New York Critic*: "she left the impression that she was the coming woman if not the coming man for the pianoforte."[34]

The accolades seemed endless—the *New York Tribune:* "She took at once a leading position among American performers."[35]

The *New York Commercial Advertiser:* "…showed herself a remarkable artist in many ways."[36]

The *New York Star:* "…she is a brilliant pianist in every sense of the term."[37]

The *New York Musical Courier:* "…as to leave no doubt in the minds of connoisseurs that she is an artist of the first rank."[38]

Her rise was meteoric.

Over the course of Adele aus der Ohe's first two seasons in America, 1886–87 and 1887–88, famed critic Henry Edward Krehbiel documented a total of no less than eighteen appearances in New York City alone.[39] In the first four months of 1887, following her December debut she appeared in New York City a total of eight times, and just during the months of March and April she performed four separate concerti. During those first few months in America she appeared with all three of the reigning conductors: Anton Seidl, Walter Damrosch, and Theodore Thomas, with the *New York Mail* noting, "Fräulein aus der Ohe, who plays at next Saturday's Philharmonic concert, will then have been heard at each of our series of important concerts..."[40]

She became a classic American "overnight success" story.

On January 8, 1887, a mere two weeks following her debut with Anton Seidl, she appeared with the Symphony Society at the Metropolitan Opera House. Walter Damrosch was conducting and the concerto on this occasion was the Chopin E minor. The *New York Herald* reported, "Fräulein aus der Ohe interpreted the Chopin concerto with such technical splendor and with such depth of feeling that one is safe in ranking her with the very best pianists that have been heard in this country..."[41]

The *New York Tribune* stated what perhaps many were thinking (or rather worrying—Could she possibly live up to all this hype?): "... Fräulein aus der Ohe made so profound an impression when she played at the first of Herr Seidl's concerts that her second appearance in public was awaited with something akin to anxiety. Between her selections on the former occasion and yesterday... there was a great difference, and it served to emphasize the conviction, which was generally expressed two weeks ago, that this young woman is a piano player of extraordinary present merit and most brilliant promise..."[42]

On February 15 she participated in a private concert at Chickering Hall where she played Chopin's *Andante Spianato and Grand Polonaise* Op. 22, the Schubert-Liszt song transcription *Gretchen am Spinnrade*, and Tausig's transcription of the Strauss waltz *Nachtfalter*.

She returned to Chickering Hall on March 2 for a benefit concert, playing a Nocturne of Chopin, the *Valse Caprice* of Rubinstein, and the Liszt Polonaise in E. On March 4 she was at Steinway Hall where she performed a lullaby by Floersheim, the *Spinnerlied* by Wagner-Liszt and Liszt's Second Hungarian Rhapsody. On March 12 she again played the Liszt E-flat Concerto, this time at the Metropolitan Opera House with Walter Damrosch conducting. Of this performance the *New York Tribune* astutely observed, "But perhaps the best and most significant tribute of all to Fräulein aus der Ohe was the warm and perfect accompaniment given to the playing of the orchestra, a natural and spontaneous result of her musicianly work."[43]

Then, on March 14, 1887, she presented her much-awaited solo debut recital at Steinway Hall. Again the press loved her:

Fräulein aus der Ohe gave a piano recital at Steinway Hall last evening to the edification of a large and appreciative audience. The task of entertaining a large assembly of people unaided is no small one, but Fräulein aus der Ohe performed it with ease and grace. Her programme was drawn from the richest treasures of piano music, and was notable for its breadth and formidable nature. It consisted of Bach's Toccata and

Fugue in D minor, arranged by Tausig, Schumann's Carnaval, two nocturnes and the C-sharp minor valse of Chopin, Mendelssohn's Spinnerlied, and a grand polonaise by Zarebski, and from the Liszt repertoire a nocturne, the Waldesrauchen, and the Rhapsodie Hongroise No. 9, known as the Pesth Carnival. The attention of the audience was at once chained by the fine interpretation of the opening number. It is seldom that a Bach fugue is so intelligently read and so brilliantly executed. The performance was perhaps the most notable of the evening, as showing the most thorough comprehension of the most severe and scholarly of composers. The Schumann Carnaval is unintelligible to all who are unacquainted with Schumann's critical writings and who have no knowledge of the personality of Eusebius and Florestan or of the fanciful society of the Davidsbündler. Those who possessed the key to its significance must have found rare enjoyment in the finished series of tone pictures which Fräulein aus der Ohe produced last evening. It was a rendering that could fairly be called in the strictest sense of the word an interpretation. In her other selections the pianist was successful, and in some of them her brilliance and power fairly carried away the audience, which throughout the evening was prolific in demonstrations of delight. [44]

The *New York Critic* added, "... the recital drew to Steinway Hall an audience almost as notable for its size as for its enthusiasm. But this is not to be wondered at, for it is many years since such masterly playing as Fräulein aus der Ohe's has been heard in a New York concert room."[45]

News of her spectacular successes in New York began to spread and she was invited to Boston. The Boston Symphony, established in 1881, is one of the oldest orchestras in the country. They were completing their sixth season of concerts when aus der Ohe first appeared with them in March 1887. The music director, one of the leading conductors of the day, was Austrian-born Wilhelm Gericke. Miss aus der Ohe and Mr. Gericke quickly developed a mutual admiration for each other and became good friends as well as musical colleagues. She first performed in Cambridge and then, on March 26, 1887, played her Boston debut with Mr. Gericke and the Boston Symphony. For this performance Adele aus der Ohe chose the Chopin Concerto in E minor, Op. 11. The Bostonians were even more ecstatic and profuse in their praise than the New Yorkers had been.

The *Evening Transcript* wrote:

> The hall was thronged as one seldom sees it, except sometimes on "Elijah" or "Messiah" nights, all available standing room being taken and the steps on each side of the stage filled with listeners... Miss aus der Ohe made a positively tremendous impression with the Chopin concerto; she is, indeed, a pianist like few, and may be ranked with those exceedingly rare birds who have not only been pupils of Liszt, but have really learnt something from him.... her technique is in every way so magnificent, that, in this respect, she may fairly be regarded as belonging to the hors concours class

[beyond competition] . . . Miss aus der Ohe's style is very simple and natural indeed, while the masterly ease, fire, grace and magnetism of her playing place her on a pinnacle which only the few elect among pianists can hope to reach. [46]

The *Boston Courier* noted, "Power and delicacy are combined in the work of this artiste, and she adds to these a perception of the composer's thoughts, an *Innigkeit* that is thoroughly German . . ."[47]

Musical Matters: "The utmost capacity of the hall was tested by the audience at both concert and rehearsal, hundreds being unable to secure even standing room . . . a technique which places her as a virtuoso alongside [Anton] Rubinstein, Von Bülow, and Essipoff, while as an interpretation it showed her to be singly sensitive to the finest and most subtle thought of her composer . . . After each movement she was applauded for many seconds . . ."[48]

The *Boston Daily Advertiser*: ". . . showed herself to be among the few really great pianists who have been here of late years. Her success was a complete conquest . . ."[49]

Music critic Max Eliot[50] announced, "The delight she gives to real music lovers is unbounded."[51]

And—in a delightfully poetic vein—critic Howard Malcom Ticknor[52] declared, "Said Lord Ipsden to his sweetheart, Lady Baroara, after Christie Johnstone, according to history, as set down in Charles Reade's novel—had rescued young Gatry from drowning: 'Yes, dearest, you have seen something great done at last, and by a woman too!' Such, in substance, was what everybody in the enormous audience which last evening attended the closing concert of this sixth season of the Boston Symphony orchestra said to his neighbor, and such was the sentiment of the tremendous applause which again and again, until five times, recalled to the platform the new pianist, Miss aus der Ohe..."[53]

Aus der Ohe was immediately engaged for the Boston Symphony's spring tour. In the early decades of its existence, the Boston Symphony toured extensively throughout the East Coast, and these tours were an excellent means of bringing orchestral music to cities that did not yet have their own orchestras. These tours were, however, fast paced. In a letter offering a suggestion as to how to contact her, aus der Ohe wrote, "send me a telegraph under the address: Care of Boston Symphony Orchestra; either Monday to Rochester, Tuesday to Syracuse, or Wednesday to Troy..."[54]

In April she returned to New York City and on April 3 she played the Mendelssohn Concerto in G minor at Steinway Hall, about which the *New York World* noted, "Fräulein aus der Ohe, the Patti[55] of the piano...was, of course, the great attraction of the evening, and her marvelous playing...called forth most enthusiastic applause."[56] *The New York Times* added, "...her rendering of the finale was full of such splendid brio, and so admirable in the fluency and distinctness of its enunciation, that it quite carried the audience away and she was compelled to repeat the movement."[57]

Aus der Ohe's final New York performance in that first wildly busy season in America was on April 8 when she played Weber's *Koncertstücke* for Piano and Orchestra with the New York Philharmonic Society conducted by Theodore Thomas. The *New York Sun* observed, "She played Weber's *Koncertstücke* in a truly noble manner, elevating its worn and sometimes trivial phrases to a height of real grandeur. Her manner, too, is exceedingly pleasing. She is quiet, attentive only to the music in progress, calm, dignified, and very sweet and genial in her way of greeting or saluting the audience."[58]

The *Star* concluded, "Fräulein aus der Ohe has merit of so high an order that it is almost hypercritical to write of her laurels of color and poetic feeling. Her power, technical ability and brilliancy are undeniable and will always insure her enthusiastic reception at the hands of even so critical an audience as the Philharmonic subscribers."[59]

Her triumph was complete and Adele and Mathilde sailed for Germany, exhausted but elated. It is little wonder that she wrote from the family home at Königstrasse 7 in Zehlendorf, a suburb of Berlin, "But coming here [home], I saw first how very much we were tired out and how necessary the change of the climate and the wonderful crossing of the ocean seemed to be for us. And so I hope it will be good for our health. Here we are living in a lovely place, near of a charming lake, dreaming and practicing. We have passed our time till now enjoying my beloved art, the nature, and the pleasure of being reunited with brother and sister. So we hope to live till some time, as I find it most agreeable..."[60] The charm of this home is evident from a letter in which aus der Ohe described a May scene to Mrs. Gilder:

Now the jessamine and rose bushes are covered with blossoms, the picture from our windows is indeed a lovely one. First our garden, then wide green fields, and finally the dark pine woods, and these are quite near to the back side of the house also. It is so quiet—peace and joyousness seem to pervade everywhere—just the very place to rest and study. I work a great deal, playing and writing, what is a main thing, of course.[61]

She had left Germany the previous fall, a little-known student of Liszt, and returned a famous concert pianist. Offers began to pour in from all over the world, and the demand to hear her remained unabated for the next twenty years.

This amazing endeavor—a young, unknown, aspiring concert pianist crossing the ocean—surely was a risk and must have been a source of worry and anxiety for her brother and sisters. With both parents already gone, there was most likely very little spare money available for Adele's career. Quite possibly it had even been necessary to borrow funds to finance the trip, a trip that carried no guarantees of success. We can only imagine the sense of relief and joy in that return, knowing that all the right decisions had been made and that the future was secure.

Aus der Ohe made a poignant remark in a letter describing her return to Germany: "We spent a short time in Berlin to visit the tombs of our parents..."[62] Her parents, despite their long lives, had, unfortunately, not lived quite long enough to see what magnificent fruits their labors had borne.

Courtesy of the Alice Marshall Women's History Collection, AKM 91/95, Archives and Special Collections at the Penn State Harrisburg Library, Pennsylvania State University Libraries

Mr. and Mrs. Gilder

Of all the many people that Adele and Mathilde met during that incredibly busy and amazingly successful first season in America, two whom they counted among their closest friends were Mr. and Mrs. Gilder.[63]

Richard Watson Gilder (1844–1909) and Helena Dekay Gilder (1846–1916) were at the hub of the literary and artistic scene in New York City when aus der Ohe arrived in 1886. Richard Gilder was a poet and editor of the *Century Magazine*, and his wife Helena was a painter. Each Friday evening of the "season" (late fall until early spring), Richard and Helena Gilder opened their home to whomever of the cultural intelligentsia happened to be in New York. These Friday evenings became very popular and were a source of inspiration and entertainment for most of the great artists and musicians of that time. Everyone who was anyone came.

American author William Ellsworth remembered,

One thing that gave great pleasure to the whole group
of young artists and literary people in my early days

in New York was that so many who were friends for life started together... Some of these men, with Mr. and Mrs. Gilder founded the Society of American Artists, the first meeting of which was held in the studio at 103 East Fifteenth Street in 1877... The Friday evenings went on when the growing Gilder family fairly burst through the walls of the little studio and moved into larger and somewhat more conventional quarters in what was then Clinton Place; the receptions (they could hardly be called that) were very simple; I suppose there must have been "refreshments," but I cannot remember anything but the people. You met Paderewski and Madame Modjeska, Duse, Jefferson, aus der Ohe, Kipling, Sargent, Cecilia Beaux[64]—they came and they found something to bear away with them. Mrs. Gilder's idea in being at home week after week was 'that people shall meet often and have something in common.' Music was, of course, what best held them together, and such music! The inspiration of many of Gilder's poems came from the music at these Friday evenings.[65]

Poet Emma Lazarus (1849–1887), whose words are famously etched into the base of the Statue of Liberty, remembered going to the Gilders one Friday evening and finding fifty people there, and American novelist Constance Cary Harrison (1843–1920) remembered, "at the house of our friends the Richard Watson Gilders, one was always sure to encounter the '*dessus du panier*' [*the crème de la crème*] of the literary and artistic world. There I first heard Adele aus der Ohe witch magic music from piano keys!"[66]

At the end of each season, Richard and Helena Gilder retreated to their beloved home in Marion for the quietness of a rural summer. As the nineteenth and early twentieth centuries became more urbanized and industrialized, many artists and literary people began to feel a nostalgia for rural life and began to move into small, rustic towns. Throughout America various informal art communities developed, and Marion, Massachusetts, about fifty miles south of Boston, was one of these. The Gilders lived in a quaint old house and used one of the outbuildings as an art studio for Mrs. Gilder. Helena Gilder invited Adele and Mathilde to Marion, but the hectic pace of that first season in America prevented them from making the trip.

From her family home in Zehlendorf, aus der Ohe wrote on July 13, 1887:

My dear Mrs. Gilder

Let me give you notice of our happily having arrived in Germany some weeks ago! Long time I intended to do so and to tell you how often my sister and I have thought back to the very pleasant and agreeable hours we . . . pass[ed] in your home in New York! I suppose that now you will have gone already to Marion and will enjoy there the being separated from all Winter Trouble! Oh how would we have enjoyed it with you, to be in that lovely spot we know so well already by description and pictures! I must say that I regret it still that the delightful view to pass there a short time in your house and family could not be realized this summer! . . .

Let me tell you still that we anticipate the pleasure

we hope to have next season: to meet you happily again and to pass again in your house hours like those we keep still in fresh remembrance and which were in fact too agreeable to be ever forgotten.

We hope, if God will, to return to America in September.

With my and my sister's best regards to you and to Mr. Gilder.

I remain yours faithfully,
Adele aus der Ohe

By September 1887, Adele and Mathilde indeed were back in America for another busy season of concerts. Aus der Ohe appeared nine times in New York City during the 1887–88 season, beginning with a solo recital at Unity Hall on October 15. The program consisted of the Sonata in C-sharp minor Op. 27 No. 2, the *Moonlight*, of Beethoven, two Scarlatti pieces and a waltz by Anton Rubinstein, a nocturne and the A-flat Ballade of Chopin, the *Symphonic Etudes* by Schumann, and she closed, as she did all her solo recitals, with Liszt. In this case it was the *Valse Oubliée* and one of her "trademark pieces," the *Spanish Rhapsody*.

She participated in a November 20 concert at the Liederkranz Hall where she played the piano solo in Beethoven's Choral Fantasy, about which the *New York Musical Courier* wrote, "The gem of the evening however...was Beethoven's Op. 80. The piano solo was magnificently played by Miss aus der Ohe."[67]

In December she was in Brooklyn where, on December 17, she performed Beethoven's Fifth Piano Concerto with

Theodore Thomas. The very next day she appeared at the Arion Hall in Brooklyn, playing Liszt's E-flat Concerto with Frank Van der Stucken conducting. Van der Stucken was an American conductor who established the Cincinnati Orchestra in 1895.

On December 20, she was at Steinway Hall with Theodore Thomas, this time performing Liszt's Second Piano Concerto in A major. On January 3, she returned to Brooklyn for another performance of Liszt's E-flat Concerto, with Walter Damrosch leading the orchestra.

She then traveled to Boston where, on January 7, she played Beethoven's Fifth Piano Concerto with Wilhelm Gericke at the podium. She returned, along with the Boston Symphony and Mr. Gericke, to New York to perform the Schumann Concerto at Steinway Hall.

Of the Schumann performance, the *New York Sun* reported, "Surely no such rendering of this magnificent piano work was ever given in New York... It was a superb and masterly performance, worthy of every commendation.... At times it seemed as though she were simply pulling the orchestra along with her...."[68]

The World reported, "This remarkable artiste has done nothing better since she has been with us..."[69]

The *New York Herald* enthused, "...she was summoned five times..."[70]

It seemed nearly impossible for the press to give adequate impressions of the frenzy her performances evoked. Of a Liszt Concerto performance the *Boston Herald* noted, "The ovation... beggars description. Everybody got worked up to the boiling point, and finally the orchestra gave vent to the enthusiasm of its members by a fanfare of trumpets and drums as the artist appeared for the fourth time to bow her thanks, after which she graciously added the Wagner *Spinning Song* as an encore number."[71]

On January 28 she appeared at the Metropolitan Opera House with Mr. Damrosch in the Rubinstein D minor Concerto. February 7 found her at the Academy of Music in Brooklyn at a private concert of the Apollo Club, performing a Rubinstein *Valse*, the Chopin *Berceuse* and the Liszt Polonaise. Her final New York performance of the season occurred March 10 of 1888 with the Philharmonic Society at the Metropolitan Opera House, Theodore Thomas conducting, in Beethoven's Concerto in E-flat—the *Emperor*.

The *New York Sun* gave the Beethoven Concerto high praise: "Fräulein aus der Ohe's artistic and scholarly interpretation...was dignified, and even reverential, in its strict attention to marks of expression, and as regards the meaning and spirit of the composer..."[72]

The *World* noted, "The Metropolitan Opera House was filled...she...was recalled six times after the close of the concerto and received the homage of her audience."[73]

Concert invitations poured in and she began to travel extensively throughout America. Following Philadelphia performances of the Liszt E-flat Concerto, *The Philadelphia Times* wrote, "She is a genuine pupil of Liszt and plays as he did, with a strong, firm, emphatic touch that gives to every note its value and its meaning..."[74]

The *Philadelphia Evening Bulletin* added, "She touches the piano as though it were hers by right. Her hands are long, and she plays with great force and virility, but technical

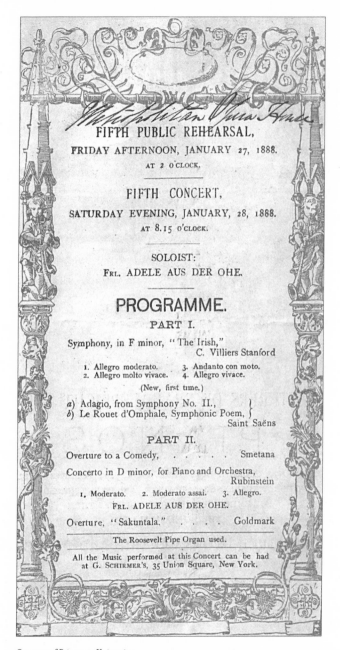

FIFTH PUBLIC REHEARSAL,

FRIDAY AFTERNOON, JANUARY 27, 1888.

AT 2 O'CLOCK,

FIFTH CONCERT,

SATURDAY EVENING, JANUARY, 28, 1888.

AT 8.15 O'CLOCK.

SOLOIST:

FRL. ADELE AUS DER OHE.

PROGRAMME.

PART I.

Symphony, in F minor, "The Irish,"
C. Villiers Stanford

1. Allegro moderato. 3. Andanto con moto.
2. Allegro molto vivace. 4. Allegro vivace.

(New, first time.)

a) Adagio, from Symphony No. II., }
b) Le Rouet d'Omphale, Symphonic Poem, }
Saint Saëns

PART II.

Overture to a Comedy, ... Smetana

Concerto in D minor, for Piano and Orchestra,
Rubinstein

1. Moderato. 2. Moderato assai. 3. Allegro.
FRL. ADELE AUS DER OHE.

Overture, "Sakuntala." . . . . Goldmark

The Roosevelt Pipe Organ used.

All the Music performed at this Concert can be had
at G. SCHIRMER'S, 35 Union Square, New York.

Courtesy of Princeton University

correctness is a matter of secondary importance, compared with fire, inspiration and soul, and these she has..."[75]

The *Chicago Morning News* announced, "Fräulein aus der Ohe is a bona fide pupil of Liszt, and has much of the dash and spirit of that master..."[76]

America had only emerged about twenty years earlier from the Civil War, and the nation was rapidly being trans-formed from a predominantly rural, agrarian society to an urbanized industrial giant. Cities throughout the country were expanding and the desire to hear music became seemingly insatiable. People everywhere were eager to hear the same musical celebrities the East Coast cities were enjoying. Orchestras were being created and organiza-tions for presenting recitals were being established. The nation's transportation system was also rapidly expanding. With the completion of the first transcontinental railroad in 1869, the rail system was now extensive enough to make possible the travel necessary to bring these musicians to the "hinterlands"—and in the case of aus der Ohe, everyone wanted to hear what all the hype was about.

On June 2, 1888, she played a recital in Ohio, at Oberlin College.

> Seldom has the Oberlin concert going public been so agog to hear any musical celebrity as in the case of Fräulein aus der Ohe, who made her first appearance here last week before a large and enthusiastic audi-ence. Our imaginations had been so heated by the fabulous reports from the cities where she has played, and particularly by the glowing description of her in the

*Century Magazine by Mr. Bagby, that we were prepared
for a great treat or a great disappointment. It is quite
unnecessary to inform any who heard the concert or the
enthusiastic description of those who did, that we were
not disappointed. The style of her playing was precisely
what we had been led to expect from the descriptions
which we had seen—brilliant, showy, clever and artistic. The programme was one remarkably well adjusted
to bring out the powers of such a pianist and it is hardly
too much to say that there was not a number on the
programme[77] that has ever been better played here . . .*

*We imagine that the impression which the hearer,
whether a musician or a music lover, would remember
longest and would single out most readily if he were
asked for his opinion of Fräulein aus der Ohe's playing,
is the sense of absolute confidence, openness, freedom,
dash, verve, brio, aplomb—give it whatever name you
can find in the polyglot jargon of musical criticism—
that characterizes her style throughout . . . There is an
appearance of ease and spontaneity about her playing
that often gives it an almost impromptu effect. When
she is playing you never set your mind critically to
examine her interpretation of the master. Fräulein aus
der Ohe does not interpret, she plays—an accomplishment as much higher as the harp of Sappho is loftier
than the scratchy goose quill of Rhadamanthos.[78] To
our mind she is by all odds the most finished concert
artist that has ever played here, and if her stay in the
Pactolian regions of America[79] continues next year, it is
hoped that she may be secured again . . .[80]*

In the summer of 1888, Adele and Mathilde made a very quick trip home to Berlin. They departed New York on July 18 and returned to New York in early September. This was an amazingly short summer vacation. The ocean crossing from New York to Berlin took nearly two weeks so they only arrived in Germany around the beginning of August. They had to already depart by the end of August (for another two-week ocean journey) in order to be back in New York by early September for a third full season of concerts, which began with a tour of the American West.

Aus der Ohe performed on October 5 in Minneapolis, Minnesota. By October 16 she was in Kansas City from where she wrote to Mrs. Gilder, "You see we are far in the West!...We left New York for a longer tour on September 29 and have been traveling since this time...We had here tonight our second and last concert and are to be tomorrow in Cedar Rapids..."[81] On October 24 she played in Omaha, Nebraska, and then returned to New York.

The year 1889 began with a solo recital in New York. The notion of a piano solo recital was still a rather new and evolving idea in the 1880s and 1890s. Public performances in the first half of the nineteenth century were essentially musical variety events. An excellent example is the program for Chopin's final public performance in Paris on February 16, 1848, at the Salle Pleyel:[82]

1. Piano Trio by Mozart with Chopin playing
   the piano part
2. Arias sung by Mlle. Antonia Molina di Mondi

3. Nocturne and Barcarolle played by Chopin
4. Aria sung by Mlle. Mondi
5. Etude and Berceuse played by Chopin
   Intermission
6. Scherzo, Adagio, and Finale from Chopin's
   Cello Sonata in G minor with Chopin playing the piano part
7. Aria sung by Gustave-Hippolyte Roger
8. Preludes, Mazurkas, and Waltz in D-flat
   Op. 64 played by Chopin

Concerts from this era always involved more than one artist and entire works were not necessarily performed. At this concert the first movement of the Cello Sonata was omitted. Also, artists often performed with the music.

Liszt completely revolutionized this. The modern-day piano recital experience was invented by Liszt. He was the first to devote the entire program to his own piano playing and the first to perform his entire programs from memory. He was the first to place the piano across the stage, allowing the audience to see his hands and profile, and allowing the lid to be raised in order to reflect the sound into the concert hall. Prior to this, the piano was typically placed so that the performer sat with his (or her) back to the audience. "The very term 'recital' was his; he introduced it in London on June 9, 1840, for a concert in the Hanover Square rooms."[83]

However, the notion of a pianist sharing the program with another artist (usually a singer) persisted until about 1900. Many of aus der Ohe's early recital programs in

America alternated sets of piano solos with vocal solos, but she gradually, following the innovative ways of her great teacher, Liszt, moved away from this format and devoted the entire evening to her own performance. Writing of her January 1889 recital, *The New York Sun* warned of the perils of these new ideas: "It is always a formidable undertaking to entertain a hall full of people for two hours with a piano. People are apt to tire of the same kind of sounds, even when produced by the greatest performer. It is therefore highly to the credit of Miss Adele aus der Ohe that she retained a very large audience in Steinway Hall last evening to the last note of her programme... Rosenthal, who was present, applauded more heartily than anyone..."[84]

Aus der Ohe and Moriz Rosenthal were longtime friends from their student days in Weimar. They were nearly exact contemporaries; Rosenthal was one year younger than aus der Ohe, having been born in 1862. He too had gone to Liszt as a child prodigy at the age of fourteen. An interesting example of aus der Ohe coming to the aid of her old friend, and in his own repertoire no less, was reported in 1897: "Adele aus der Ohe is filling the engagements that Moriz Rosenthal, the pianist, was obliged to cancel because of his unfortunate illness. She is playing the same pieces that he was to have played."[85]

The *Metropolitan Magazine* of New York, in an 1899 article, compared the two great pianists. "It is something of a luxury to enjoy in the same season the presence of two such artists as Moriz Rosenthal and Adele aus der Ohe. The one represents the interpretation of a vigorous, manly soul and a keen analytical mind delivering themselves with authority. The other reveals the hidden fires of a nature, deeply poetical and even mystical, rising at times to heights of passionate intensity."[86]

The *St Paul Daily Globe*, in writing about her January 16, 1889, recital in Minnesota, provided a sense of the depth and profundity of aus der Ohe's interpretations: "...as she sits at the piano, her expressive face reflecting the light and shade of the music her deft fingers produce, her audience suspects that she is not playing to them, but to the spirit of the genius she is giving form..."[87]

The year 1889 continued with February concerts in Boston. She commenced a spring tour with a concert at the Brooklyn Academy of Music on March 26 and pro-

Moriz Rosenthal, Adele aus der Ohe, and Franz Liszt (note the size of her hands)

Courtesy of David Cannata and Rena Charnin Mueller

ceeded on to Philadelphia, Pittsburgh, Washington D.C., Baltimore, and other cities.

The pace must have been frenetic and while exhilarating, also, very likely, exhausting. A letter of April 1889 to Mrs. Gilder: "We leave this afternoon for Toronto, Buffalo, etc. and I do not know exactly which day we may be back! I confess that my concerts have kept us this season in an almost cruel manner from seeing our friends...Possibly we will be here [New York] some days in the week before Easter. With the exception of these days, the rest of the season appears to keep me rather busy, as after Easter there begins a long series of music festivals which perhaps may give us some times a chance of being one day in New York..."[88]

By June she was touring the American South. In a letter mailed from Memphis, Tennessee, she wrote, "We are always still traveling and far in the South now, as you see. Hot weather becomes more frequent now and we begin to long for the close of this season. Still it has been very delightful till now and I hope sincerely that it will continue in the same way till to the last concert of this busy season. My work of the last seven weeks was all done on music festivals (except a few other concerts) and they were all fine occasions, where to play gave me true pleasure. I tried to make people forget their heavy 'woe' for some moments. Did I succeed? I hope so, believing firmly that true endeavours will at least sometimes not be quite in vain...We expect to return to New York by Sunday next, after visiting some cities farther north, Louisville, Cleveland, Rochester, etc..."[89]

The summer of 1889 allowed for another brief return to Germany. Adele and Mathilde departed New York on June 27 and by September they were once again back in America for a fourth season, beginning on September 27, 1889, with Beethoven's *Emperor* Concerto at the Worcester Music Festival in Massachusetts.

In November she performed the Rubinstein Concerto No. 3 in G major with Theodore Thomas for the Philharmonic Society's opening concert of the season. The *New York Sun* reported, "Her ease of movement, celerity, and certainty in bravura passages are splendid, not only to hear but to see. For Miss aus der Ohe is extremely graceful in the management of her hands, fingers, and arms. Never has a better concert been heard from this renowned society than that of last night. No more charming or artistic soloist than Miss aus der Ohe can be found . . . More of praise could not be said."[90]

She played the Rubinstein G major Concerto in December in Boston with the legendary Arthur Nikisch conducting. Arthur Nikisch was in his first year as music director of the Boston Symphony. Wilhelm Gericke had returned to Europe and Nikisch had been named as his successor. (Nikisch would also, in a few years, return to Europe to become director of the Leipzig Gewandhaus Orchestra and then later the Principal Conductor of the Berlin Philharmonic.)

The Beacon reported, "There is surely no pianist in this country who enjoys a greater general favor than Miss Adele aus der Ohe."[91]

The Boston Evening Transcript: ". . . counted among the 'events' of the winter."[92]

The Boston Sunday Herald: ". . . at the front of the pianists of today . . ."[93]

The Boston Daily Traveler: ". . . best achievement in Boston."[94]

The Boston Daily Advertiser: ". . . never appeared to better advantage . . . The recalls . . . were evidence that the large audience understood the worth of the performance."[95]

And *The Boston Times*: "She was more liberally applauded than any soloist this season."[96]

To put this last statement into perspective, other soloists appearing with the Boston Symphony that season included such keyboard luminaries as the Hungarian pianist (and fellow Liszt student) Rafael Joseffy; the American pianist (and Lescheitzky student) Fanny Bloomfield-Zeisler; and aus der Ohe's friend and fellow Weimar classmate, the Polish pianist Moriz Rosenthal.

The whirlwind life she was enjoying must have been exciting. It was impossible to fit it all in! A letter to Mrs. Gilder declined a dinner invitation, saying, "...we felt too tired out after a night's journey and very tiresome preceding days to go out anymore. But we felt very bad about it and missed greatly the pleasure of an evening in your home."[97]

In reviewing a Pittsburgh recital, the *Pittsburgh Dispatch* wrote on February 14, 1890, "In Liszt's big bombastic *Spanish Rhapsody* Miss aus der Ohe proved her right to be considered—as was the fact—Liszt's favorite pupil among his favorite sex. Indeed, for this performance, the sex qualification may be omitted. D'Albert, himself, could not have conquered the abounding difficulties of this piece with a more electrifying virtuosity in all particulars. More could not be said."[98] The prevalence of this type of comment in the writings of the nineteenth century is unsettling. The sex bias that was accepted without question in aus der Ohe's time strikes the modern-day reader as blatantly unfair. Pianists were divided by their sex, and comparisons almost always remained within this division. Too much of the recognition aus der Ohe received was qualified by the fact that she was (only) a woman. It is irritating to constantly read this bias and one can very well imagine it was annoying to aus der Ohe as well. It seemed the highest praise a woman could possibly receive was to be compared to a man!

An almost rapturous article appeared in the University of Michigan school newspaper, *The Chronicle*, following her recital[99] on February 26, 1890, in Ann Arbor. It gives a sense of the intensity of the feelings aus der Ohe's audiences had for her. There was a deep respect and reverence for her as a musician, as well as a genuine love for her as a person.

One of the finest audiences ever seen in University Hall assembled last Wednesday evening to hear the distinguished pianist, Miss Adele aus der Ohe, of whom it may truly be said that she is an artist by the "Grace of God." Her first appearance on the stage was the signal for enthusiastic applause, for in her bearing could be discerned that consciousness of mastery which prepares an audience for perfect enjoyment, and her singularly sweet and simple manner, which makes the woman no less attractive than the artiste, won all hearts at once . . .

. . . She is more than realizing all that the great master, Franz Liszt, expected of her . . . Every one present at this memorable concert must have been impressed with the purity, nobility, and tenderness of her conceptions, and the brilliancy and accuracy of her technique, which made it possible for her to interpret a programme of such varied character in so masterly a manner. As to writing criticism of her performance, it is simply impossible. In Beethoven, classical and broad; in Scarlatti, Paderewski, and Raff, sympathetic and forceful; in Chopin, tender, passionate, and soulful;

in Liszt, brilliant, sparkling and fiery. The whole pro-
gramme was so perfectly played that admiration and
reverence for such wonderful talent must take the place
of criticism. It is a delight to be taken out of a critical
state occasionally, and to give one's self over to pure
enjoyment. And the record of Miss aus der Ohe has
been that she, as few others, can arouse such genuine
enthusiasm (not over her playing alone, but over the
music played) that criticism is not in order. She was
delighted with her reception, and we are confident that
each one in the audience has a warm feeling toward
the artiste who could give such genuine and unalloyed
pleasure—and at the same time make one better for
having been taken out of themselves.[100]

She must have been practically re-engaged on the
spot because by November of that same year she returned
for another recital.[101] She performed at the University of
Michigan twice more—in January 1899[102] and one final
concert in March 1904.[103]

On March 8, 1890, in Chicago, she played a recital
that was certainly a novelty in those days and is still quite
unusual: "...the program consisted entirely of compositions and transcriptions of Franz Liszt"[104] The works she
performed included the Polonaise in E major, the *Valse
Oubliée* and *Mephisto Waltz* No. 2, Liszt's Nocturne, three
Wagner transcriptions, including *Isolde's Love Death*, the
Spanish Rhapsody, and the *Tarantelle di Bravura.*

She traveled to Minnesota for a recital in Minneapolis
on March 12 and a concerto performance on March 18 in

St. Paul. The concerto was played with a group of musicians called the Danz Orchestra. The Minneapolis Symphony (later renamed The Minnesota Orchestra) would not be founded until 1903 by Munich-born Emil Oberhoffer. Aus der Ohe would return to Minnesota to help inaugurate this fine organization by performing the Liszt E-flat Concerto with them on January 29, 1904, the second concert of their first season.

A letter from Minneapolis notes, "We have been awfully busy all the time...but enjoyed greatly traveling, playing, etc..."[105] But even aus der Ohe's incredible stamina was tried by the northern cold; and in the same letter she continues, "...we both [she and Mathilde] cannot very well stand the climate here and should greatly like to run away from the cold regions, if we were not obligated to stay a few days longer on account of my playing in St. Paul on Tuesday next. We seldom experienced such cold as there was yesterday in spite of bright sunshine."

By her fifth season in America her travels spanned the entire continent. Her first appearance on the West Coast was in San Francisco on November 18, 1890. *The San Francisco Morning Call* reported the following day:

> *The lovers of music in San Francisco—and their name is legion—turned out last night on the occasion of the first appearance here of Adele aus der Ohe...Irving Hall was filled upon this occasion with the largest audience ever assembled in this city to listen to a piano recital...their appreciation of her marked ability was demonstrated by repeated calls after each number. In*

fact, their admiration outran their discretion, and the
unusually warm welcome and the encores demanded
rather taxed the nerves and the strength of the charming
young debutante. However, it was a regular California
greeting...[106]

At her second appearance in San Francisco, she played
the Liszt E-flat Concerto with "the assistance of an orchestra numbering thirty-five pieces under the direction of
Professor J. H. Rosewald."[107] As in Minneapolis, she was
far ahead of any organized professional orchestra. The San
Francisco Symphony would not be founded until 1911 and
by then aus der Ohe was no longer performing in America.

Again, the *Morning Call* related:

... the immense success of her performance at Irving Hall
yesterday afternoon established for all time to come her
reputation in this city as a virtuoso who may possibly
be equaled, but who it will be difficult to believe can be
excelled. When ladies pay the grand tribute of rising in
their seats and waving their handkerchiefs in token of
their appreciation it may be regarded as a fixed fact that
the genuineness of their emotions has been stirred by
something out of the ordinary course of events ... and no
wonder her emotions nearly overcame her.[108] *There are*
those who make bold to say that Adele aus der Ohe, as a
pianist, stands today without a living peer.[109]

On November 30 it was announced, "Her afternoon
and evening piano recitals have been so well attended that

two additional matinees are arranged..."[110] Aus der Ohe
played a total of six public performances in San Francisco
in that single month of November 1890.

AMUSEMENTS.

FAREWELL CHANCE TO HEAR
ADELE AUS DER OHE
"AMERICA'S GREATEST PIANISTE."
"The Best Lady Piano Virtuoso Ever Heard Here."
——POSITIVELY——
◆FINAL CONCERT IN SAN FRANCISCO➤

——IRVING HALL——

"A wonderful performer."
"What remarkable playing."
"A really rare treat."

LAST ORCHESTRAL MATINEE
Friday Afternoon, November 28, 1890.
Admission $1. Secured Seat $1 50 (H. C.)

Free List Entirely Suspended.

☞ TICKETS NOW ON SALE ☜
At Matthias Gray Co.'s, 206 and 208 Post street.
no21 tf

The Morning Call, San Francisco, Friday, November 28, 1890

In December she proceeded to "Oakland, San Jose,
Los Angeles, San Diego, and the cities of the south."[111] *The
Los Angeles Times* announced her arrival under the almost
breathlessly giddy headline, "AUS DER OHE COMING,"
and then followed up after the concert:

> *By the time she had finished the Chopin Polonaise she
> had won every heart in the house that loved music or*

appreciated real genius, and her recall was of a char-
acter to delight even an artist's soul . . . She has a way
of looking up from the piano for an instant that is as
charming as it is unconscious, and likens her to St.
Cecilia listening to heavenly harmonies . . .[112]

In 1890 Theodore Thomas was invited to Chicago to organize an orchestra for the enjoyment of the citizens of that great city. Charles Norman Fay, a prominent Chicago businessman, asked Thomas, "Would you come to Chicago if we gave you a permanent orchestra?" Thomas jumped at the chance: "I would go to Hell if they gave me a permanent orchestra."[113]

By 1891, plans were in place and Theodore Thomas departed for the Midwest to establish one of the great orchestras of the world, the Chicago Symphony. For his New York farewell performance he enlisted the help of his friend and fellow Hanoverian. "He made his last bow at the Philhar-monic concert of April 11, 1891, when he was bidden good-bye with much applause, cheers, waving of handkerchiefs, and flowers. The program consisted of . . . Schumann's Piano Concerto . . . Adele aus der Ohe was the soloist . . ."[114]

Later that fall, as the Chicago Symphony embarked upon its first season, Theodore Thomas introduced his old friend to his new orchestra. Adele aus der Ohe played the Rubinstein Concerto No. 3 in G major on February 6, 1892, with the newly formed Chicago Symphony as part of their inaugural season.

America loved aus der Ohe and she requited that love. In 1889 she wrote, "In the beginning of September we have got to be back in this country, which I always admired but which is very dear to me now."[115] And a few weeks later: "We wanted very much to stay in America this summer."[116] From another letter: "And then the parting from America—you cannot think how sad I felt when we left, and the shores so very dear to me gradually passed out of sight..."[117]

A glimpse into the tremendous financial success aus der Ohe enjoyed in addition to her artistic success comes from an entry Tchaikovsky made in his diary during his trip to America in 1891. "Reno [Tchaikovsky's American manager] gave me some interesting details about aus der Ohe's American career. She came here four years ago without a penny in her pocket, but secured an invitation to play Liszt's Concerto in the Symphony Society. Her playing was well liked; invitations poured down from everywhere; everywhere a great success accompanied her; for four years she roamed from city to city, all over America, and now she has a capital of half-a-million marks! Such is America!"[118]

It was rumored that she was the highest-paid pianist in America, and one wit, in considering the number of performances she played and the scope of her repertoire, quipped, "She deserves it!"

By the fall of 1891, as she began her sixth season in America, aus der Ohe's fame and popularity were enormous. It was also in that fall of 1891 that another pianist who was to become the epitome of late nineteenth and early twentieth century piano playing made his American debut. The great Polish pianist Ignace Paderewski, on November 17, 1891, played his first American concert in the new Carnegie Hall, which Tchaikovsky and aus der Ohe had so famously opened only six months earlier. Of Paderewski's performances the critics often were lukewarm, but the audiences went wild.

The similarities between the careers of Adele aus der Ohe and Ignace Paderewski were striking. There was only a four-month age difference—Paderewski was born in November of 1860 and aus der Ohe in February of 1861. Both had become hugely popular after spectacular debut performances. Both toured extensively and to great acclaim—and both earned large sums of money! An 1893 *Los Angeles Times* article even lamented, "Aus der Ohe is the only great pianist who will visit us this season, Paderewski having decided not to come to the Pacific Coast."[119]

Their careers differed, however, in one notable aspect. Paderewski, as well as nearly every other pianist, made his fame in Europe prior to his arrival in America. Aus der Ohe, however, was really the very earliest pianist to make her career first in America, and only after spectacular American successes did she consolidate her career with triumphs in Europe.

Eugene d'Albert, slightly younger than both aus der Ohe and Paderewski, having been born in 1864, was another who was hugely popular during the final decades of the nineteenth century. There were, of course, many widely known pianists, but these three—aus der Ohe, Paderewski, and d'Albert—were among the most famous and most popular.

The public furiously debated the issue of who was the greatest. The discussions became so heated that by 1899 the *New York Times* felt compelled to enter the fray. (The article was considered so apropos that it was later reprinted in the *Los Angeles Times*.)

> *It really does not matter who is the greatest living pianist. The only question is who is worth hearing? And Mr. Paderewski is not the only one. The American habit is to try to find out who is the best and then to refuse to go to hear any other. It is a remnant of our Yankee origin, this habit, for it is only an attempt to save money.*
>
> *Every artist, who has risen to sufficient distinction to claim the public attention has something which none of the others have. Each one has some element of personality which has differentiated him from the crowd, and it is the possession of this that has made him eminent. You may go to hear every pianist in the world except d'Albert, without hearing what d'Albert will play to you. Behind the art lies the man. The interpretive artist must of necessity read something of himself into every composition that he plays. No man would say that Mr. Mansfield's Richard III was enough. He would ask you if you had seen that of Edwin Booth. The Juliet of Julia Dean was one thing, that of Adelaide Neilson another, but both of them were in Shakespeare.*
>
> *Adele aus der Ohe does not play the Emperor Concerto as d'Albert plays it, but that is no reason why you should not hear both. Neither of these artists exhausts Beethoven. That is one of the lovely things about works of genius. They lend themselves to touches of different personalities, without losing their own identity. Therefore I say it is folly to try to find out who is the greatest*

pianist in the world. You cannot get a compendium of
the music of the piano out of any one man or woman.
No actor is the epitome of dramatic literature. The
harvest is large, and the reapers are many. Is not the
laborer worthy of his hire?[120]

Aus der Ohe and Paderewski were friends. Polish writer Maja Trochimczyk referred to "Paderewski's friend Adele aus der Ohe"[121] in one of her articles. Paderewski's longtime friend and student Zygmunt Stojowski dedicated one of his compositions to aus der Ohe, and aus der Ohe occasionally included Paderewski's music in her recital programs. Richard Gilder, one of aus der Ohe's most loyal friends, published articles promoting Paderewski's career, and aus der Ohe and Paderewski were both visitors to the Gilder home for their "Friday Evening" socials.

Aus der Ohe's friendship with the Gilders was an important one for her, and perhaps we can guess at the dynamics that made this relationship so meaningful. When Adele and Mathilde arrived in America in late 1886, Mr. and Mrs. Gilder were in their early forties while Adele was only twenty-five. It is not too difficult to see that, in addition to a friendship based on their mutual literary and artistic interests, Adele and Mathilde might also have looked to these two lovely people for the parental guidance that a young lady and her sister, in a foreign land an ocean away from family and friends, might yearn for. Adele and Mrs. Gilder even shared the same February 11 birthday.

In 1887 Richard Gilder published a volume of poetry entitled *Lyrics and Other Poems*. Included in this volume is a poem bearing the title, "Adele aus der Ohe."[122] This lovely poem, in celebration of her interpretations of Liszt and Chopin, was surely inspired, at least partially, by those exhilarating Friday evenings he and his wife hosted to the great delight and enjoyment of so many of the finest writers, painters, and musicians of the time.

Adele aus der Ohe

(LISZT)

I

What is her playing like?
'Tis like the wind in wintery northern valleys.
A dream-pause;—then it rallies
And once more bends the pine tops, suddenly shatters
the ice-crags, whitely scatters
the spray along the paths of avalanches,
startles the blood, and every visage blanches.

II

Half sleeps the wind above a swirling pool
That holds the trembling shadow of the trees;
Where waves too wildly rush to freeze
Though all the air is cool;
And hear, oh hear, while musically call
With nearer tinkling sounds, or distant roar,
Voices of fall on fall;
And now a swelling blast, that dies; and now no more,
no more.

(CHOPIN)

I

Ah, what celestial art!
And can sweet thoughts become pure tone and float,
All music, note by note,
into the tranced mind and quivering heart!
Her hand scarce stirs the singing, wiry metal—
Hear from the wild-rose fall each perfect petal!

II

And can we have, on earth, of heaven the whole,
Or be to heaven upcaught,
Hearing the soul of inexpressible thought,
Roses of sound
That strew melodious leaves upon the silent ground;
And music that is music's very soul,
Without one touch of earth,
Too tender, even for sorrow, and too bright for mirth!

Inscription: To Mr. and Mrs. Theodore Thomas with heartfelt
greetings from Adele aus der Ohe. New York, March [18]94.
Courtesy of The Newberry Library, Chicago, Illinois

Tchaikovsky and Carnegie Hall

In the last decade of the nineteenth century and the first decade of the twentieth, if one encountered a sentence that contained the words "Tchaikovsky" and "concerto," it would almost invariably end with the phrase "played by aus der Ohe." In fact in 1906 a critic for the *New York Times* stated, "Miss Adele aus der Ohe . . . has a sort of prescriptive right of possession in Tchaikovsky's First Concerto, which she has played here many times, and on one memorable occasion under the composer's own baton . . ."[123]

It is difficult from our twenty-first-century vantage to even conceive of the Tchaikovsky Concerto as having once been "new" music, but new it indeed was when aus der Ohe gave her first performance of it in 1891—it was a mere seventeen years old and the final revisions had been made only about two-and-a-half years earlier.

Tchaikovsky's Concerto No. 1 in B-flat minor is now, of course, one of the most popular and beloved of all piano concertos, but it had a rough start. The concerto might never have appeared at all—or might have appeared in a hugely altered form—had Tchaikovsky been less tenacious. Tchaikovsky was encouraged by Nicholas Rubinstein to write a piano concerto. Nicholas Rubinstein was director of the Moscow Conservatory and was a fine pianist in his own right, in addition to being the brother of the great piano virtuoso, Anton Rubinstein. The concerto was composed during the winter of 1874 and Tchaikovsky decided to dedicate it to Nicholas. Writing from San Remo, Italy, on February 2, 1878, Tchaikovsky tells the story himself:

> *In December, 1874, I had written a pianoforte concerto. As I am not a pianist, it was necessary to consult some virtuoso as to what might be ineffective, impracticable, and ungrateful in my technique. I needed a severe, but at the same time friendly, critic to point out in my work these external blemishes only. Without going into details, I must mention the fact that some inward voice warned me against the choice of Nicolas Rubinstein as a judge of the technical side of my composition. However, as he was not only the best pianist in Moscow, but also a first-rate all-around musician, and knowing that he would be deeply offended if he heard that I had taken my concerto to anyone else, I decided to ask him to hear the work and give me his opinion upon the solo parts.*
>
> *It was on Christmas Eve, 1874. We were invited to Albrecht's house, and, before we went, Nicholas Rubinstein proposed I should meet him in one of the classrooms at the Conservatoire to go through the concerto. I arrived with my manuscript, and Rubinstein and Hubert soon appeared. The latter is a very worthy, clever*

man, but without the least self-assertion. Moreover, he is exceedingly garrulous, and needs a string of words to say "yes" or "no." He is incapable of giving his opinion in any decisive form, and generally lets himself be pulled over to the strongest side. I must add, however, that this is not from cowardice, but merely from lack of character.

I played the first movement. Never a word, never a single remark. Do you know the awkward and ridiculous sensation of putting a meal before a friend, which you have cooked yourself, which he eats—and holds his tongue? Oh for a single word, for friendly abuse, for anything to break the silence! For God's sake, say something! But Rubinstein never opened his lips. He was preparing his thunderbolt, and Hubert was waiting to see which way the wind would blow. I did not require a judgment of my work from the artistic side; simply from the technical point of view. Rubinstein's silence was eloquent. "My dear friend" he seemed to be saying to himself, "how can I speak of the details when the work itself goes entirely against the grain?" I gathered patience and played the concerto straight through to the end. Still silence.

"Well?" I asked, and rose from the piano. Then a torrent broke from Rubinstein's lips. Gentle at first, gathering volume as it proceeded and finally bursting into the fury of Jupiter-Tonans. My concerto was worthless, absolutely unplayable; passages so broken, so disconnected, so unskillfully written, that they could not even be improved; the work itself was bad, trivial, common; here and there I had stolen from other

people; only one or two pages were worth anything; all
the rest had better be destroyed or entirely rewritten.
"For instance, that? And what meaning is there in
this?" Here the passages were caricatured on the piano.
"And look there! Is it possible that anyone could?" etc.,
etc., etc. But the chief thing I cannot reproduce: the tone
in which all this was said.

An independent witness of this scene must have
concluded I was a talentless maniac, a scribbler with
no notion of composing who had ventured to lay his
rubbish before a famous man. Hubert was quite overcome by my silence, and was surprised, no doubt, that
a man who had already written so many works and
was professor of composition at the Conservatoire,
could listen calmly and without contradiction to such
a jobation, such as one would hardly venture to address
a student before having gone through his work very
carefully. Then he began to comment upon Rubinstein's
criticism, and to agree with it, although he made some
attempt to soften the harshness of his judgment.

I was not only astounded, but deeply mortified, by
the whole scene. I require friendly counsel and criticism;
I shall always be glad of it, but there was no trace of
friendliness to the whole proceedings. It was a censure
delivered in such a form that it cut me to the quick. I left
the room without a word and went upstairs: I could not
have spoken for anger and agitation. Presently Rubinstein came to me and, seeing how upset I was, called
me into another room. There he repeated that my concerto was impossible, pointed out many places where it

needed to be completely revised, and said if I would suit the concerto to his requirements, he would bring it out at his concert. "I shall not alter a single note," I replied. "I shall publish the work precisely as it stands!" This intention I actually carried out.[124]

The dedication to Rubinstein was quickly replaced by a dedication to Hans von Bülow, and Mr. von Bülow played the world premiere of the Tchaikovsky Concerto on October 25, 1875, in Boston. Tchaikovsky subsequently revised the concerto twice, in the summer of 1879 and again in December of 1888. This last revision, published in 1889, is the version we now know and love and was the version aus der Ohe performed in May of 1891 at what was without a doubt the single most important performance of her entire career—the opening of Carnegie Hall. Of all the dazzling accomplishments and all the brilliant successes of her life, this was the event that secured her a permanent place in music history.

It would be hard to overemphasize the significance of the inauguration, during the first week of May 1891, of Mr. Carnegie's new concert hall. This was one of the defining moments in American music history. America was becoming wealthy and sophisticated and New York City was at the very hub of this newfound wealth and sophistication. A large, new concert hall was needed to put American culture and arts on a par with that of the great capitals of Europe. To this end, Andrew Carnegie was called upon and the hall was built. To celebrate the opening in a truly grand manner, an entire week of festivities was planned. The culmi-

nating event occurred Saturday afternoon, May 9, 1891—a
grand concert conducted by, excepting Brahms, the most
famous musician alive, Peter Ilyich Tchaikovsky, and fea-
turing several of his own compositions, most notably his
Piano Concerto in B-flat minor with Adele aus der Ohe,
one of the most famous pianists of the day, as the soloist.

It is not too difficult to sense the excitement of this concert, even now, more than one hundred years later. Picture
a lovely afternoon in early May, the audience making their
way up the steps and into the front foyer where nearly every
surface was covered in shining marble, and then entering
that grand hall for the very first time—entering into what
was by many estimates the greatest concert hall of the day,
and has remained to this day one of the great concert halls
of the world. One can almost smell the fresh plaster and
paint and feel the newly upholstered red velvet seats. People were probably nearly breathless with excitement as the
young (she had just celebrated her thirtieth birthday a few
months earlier) and already famous pianist and the older,
world-renowned Russian conductor entered the stage and
made their way to their respective places. After what was
probably a roar of applause as the two musicians appeared,
one can almost hear the hush that fell over the audience in
anticipation of the grand music they were about to hear. It
is likely that many in the audience were hearing this exciting concerto for the very first time.

Then it began—the lush, sweeping opening theme in
the orchestra, alone at first, but soon accompanied by those
huge crashing chords from the piano—it was like no other

concerto ever written. Did the audience know they were experiencing musical history in the making? Did Tchaikovsky realize that his troubled concerto was already being hailed as one of the most beloved of all time? Did aus der Ohe sense that she was giving the most important performance of her life?

Of the performance, Tchaikovsky was pleased. In his diary entry for May 9, he wrote, "My concerto went magnificently, thanks to aus der Ohe's brilliant interpretation. The enthusiasm was far greater than anything I have met with, even in Russia. I was recalled over and over..."[125]

The *New York Times* noted that "Tchaikovsky and the pianist were recalled half a dozen times, Miss aus der Ohe showing the most charming modesty and tact in her refusal to accept any of the applause for herself."[126]

Tchaikovsky quickly became a superstar during his time in America. He was constantly being interviewed, and newspapers ran stories and photos almost daily of the great musician. Young composers brought their scores for his approval and young performers were brought to play for him. Children's books describing his journey were written. In fact the "Tchaikovsky in America" mania has never really subsided—even today there are numerous books, compact discs, and even interactive video games related to this historic visit.

Aus der Ohe and Tchaikovsky became good friends. They attended numerous social events together and often dined together. They also reprised their historic New York performance twice more prior to Tchaikovsky's departure back to Russia. On May 15 they performed in Baltimore and on May 18 in Philadelphia.

One might think these May performances with Tchaikovsky would be excitement enough for aus der Ohe for one month, but no—after their May 9 Carnegie Hall concert, while Tchaikovsky took time to travel to Niagara Falls for some sightseeing, she managed to squeeze in a performance of the Liszt E-flat Concerto in Richmond, Virginia, on May 12, and a performance of the Tchaikovsky Concerto with the Boston Symphony's touring orchestra in Washington D.C., Victor Herbert conducting, on May 14, before reuniting with Tchaikovsky in Baltimore on the fifteenth.

Baltimore was the home of the Knabe piano company which produced very high-quality instruments, rivaled only by Chickering and Steinway. An amusing description of Tchaikovsky and aus der Ohe's time in Baltimore was provided by James Bartel, a classical radio host in Southern California.[127]

In 1891, Ernest Knabe proposed to add an extravagant touch to the opening ceremonies of the nation's most auspicious new musical showcase, Carnegie Hall. The Knabe firm, he announced, would finance the appearance of Peter Ilyich Tchaikovsky, widely considered the world's greatest living composer. The white-haired Russian master was initially unaware that his trip had been financed specifically by Knabe. Upon arriving in New York he was surprised to learn that after his four Carnegie Hall concerts he was expected to conduct another concert in, of all places, Baltimore.

Tchaikovsky was exhausted from two weeks of work and sightseeing by the time he boarded a Pullman for the all-night trip to Baltimore. He lay sprawled across the bed in his cabin, fully clothed. "I had no strength to undress," he told his diary.

At dawn the train pulled into Calvert Station and Tchaikovsky was taken to the St. James Hotel at Charles and Center, where, despite the hotel's advertised "European Plan," he was received, as he said, "with cold neglect." He slept, breakfasted, and walked through a drizzle to Albaugh's Lyceum Theater for rehearsal. To his dismay, he found the orchestra—the touring Boston Festival Orchestra led by Victor Herbert—under-manned, fatigued, and under-rehearsed. "Only four first violins," Tchaikovsky complained, "and the orchestra did not know my Third Suite. Mr. Herbert had not even played it through, although it had been promised that this should be done." In place of the Third Suite, Tchaikovsky substituted the easier Serenade for Strings. His First Piano Concerto was also rehearsed (on a Knabe grand, of course), with the young pianist Adele aus der Ohe, a former pupil of Liszt, who had successfully performed the work with Tchaikovsky in New York. "The orchestra was impatient," Tchaikovsky lamented. "The young concertmaster behaved in a rather tactless way, and made it too clearly evident that he thought it time to stop." Tchaikovsky had just enough time to return in the rain to the hotel and dress in his performance frock coat. The two o'clock matinee was far from sold out. The Baltimore Sun reported, "None but musical people were present." Ticket prices ranged from $1 to $1.50. In addition to Tchaikovsky's works, the overture to Weber's opera Der Freischutz and a few miniatures by Victor Herbert were played, led by Herbert. For one critic, these latter occasioned the only sour notes of the concert. He called them "a bunch of scrappy selections." Otherwise, as local newspapers described, "The Greatest Composer Living" and his music were received by the audience with applause that broke into cheers. Tchaikovsky, relatively new to conducting and still somewhat awkward on stage, acknowledged the ovations by making curt bows. Following the Piano Concerto, he was recalled five times, and each time tried to hide behind aus der Ohe (whose name had been accidentally omitted from the program). In a letter home, Tchaikovsky later offered grudging praise for the orchestra, which despite the poor rehearsal he thought played "quite well. [But] I didn't sense any special delight in the audience, at least in comparison with New York."

After the concert, Tchaikovsky had no sooner changed clothes back at the hotel when he was visited by "a Mr. Knabe," whom he described as a man of colossal girth and hospitality. Ernest shepherded the great composer to a feast at his own home, where a choice company of two dozen Baltimoreans were in attendance, including the director of the Peabody Conservatory and the Sun music critic, as well as Adele aus der Ohe and her sister. The food that night, according to Tchaikovsky, would be the finest served him in America. "Terribly delicious," he noted. Ernest zealously kept the *wine coming. The meal was followed by conversation, tricks, music, and smoking and drinking. A young local composer named Richard Burmeister foisted his own music upon Tchaikovsky by taking a place at one of the famous Knabe square pianos and playing his own piano concerto. Tchaikovsky politely did not comment.*

The evening carried on long after Tchaikovsky had tired of enjoying himself. "A terrible hatred of everything seemed to come over me." Finally after midnight, l'affaire ground to an end and Knabe escorted Tchaikovsky back to the St. James. "I slumped down on my bed like a sheaf of wheat and at once fell dead asleep," Tchaikovsky reported.

Next morning Knabe arrived uninvited at Tchaikovsky's room to take him to see the city's sights. Tchaikovsky was feeling "the peculiar American morning fatigue" that had plagued him since arriving in this country, and wanted nothing at all to do with the exuberant Knabe. But when he learned that they were being joined by aus der Ohe and her sister (a lawyer named Mr. Sutro also came along), Tchaikovsky acquiesced.

It was rainy. The first stop, naturally, was the Wm. Knabe & Co. Piano Manufactory, which had grown to become third largest in the world. The main building rose five stories above Eutaw Street and was connected by a bridge over West to a second structure four stories high. "We inspected the whole enormous piano plant in every detail," said Tchaikovsky. Transportation between floors was by steam elevators. The boiler building housed what one journalist called "one of the most beautiful and perfect engines in the country, of about 35 horsepower." It had recently won the Gold Medal at the Maryland Institute Exhibition. A labyrinthine system of steam-pipes distributed heat to the large rooms filled with heavy machinery, and to varnishing rooms, finishing rooms and drying rooms where 200,000 feet of lumber dehydrated at a constant 140 degrees. The adjoining yards contained one million feet of lumber, undergoing nine years of seasoning in all types of weather.

Tchaikovsky was impressed by the large planing machines and jointing machines, the circular saws, the lathes and drills. But of all he admired the industrious spirit of the manufactory. "The sight of so many workers with serious, intelligent faces, so clean and carefully dressed despite the manual labor, leaves a fine impression."

Lunch and champagne followed the downtown tour, then Tchaikovsky bid Ernest Knabe goodbye and boarded the train for Washington. Ernest promptly shipped a Knabe square piano to Tchaikovsky's country house at Klin, Russia. [128]

The two famous musicians traveled to Philadelphia for their final American concert together on May 18. "...as soon as he was seen in the wings conducting Miss Adele aus der Ohe upon the stage a storm of applause burst from all parts of the house, which the composer acknowledged gracefully, although with the modesty of a schoolboy. From that moment, audience, orchestra, and soloist seemed to realize that they were in the presence of genius, and Miss aus der Ohe rendered the composer's concerto with such artistic merit that her numerous admirers had ample cause to think that she excelled any of her previous efforts before an American audience."[129]

Tchaikovsky and aus der Ohe returned to New York, where they were treated to one final magnificent banquet—a dinner given in his honor at the Metropolitan Opera House by the Composer's Club. The next day: "I called on aus der Ohe and bid farewell to them [Adele and Mathilde]...Since the ship is leaving at 5:00 A.M. I must board it in the evening...heard the ship starting out at 5:00...Came out of my cabin when we passed the Statue of Liberty."[130]

He had been in America less than a month, yet his influence would be felt for generations.

Aus der Ohe must have felt a great love of and had a great affinity for the Tchaikovsky Concerto—it quickly became one of the favorite concertos in her repertoire and she was frequently asked to perform it throughout her career.

Following her performance of the concerto at a Young People's Popular Concert with the Boston Symphony on January 6, 1892, Bostonian music critics were unanimous in their praise, not only of the performance but of the composition itself.

> It was a great pleasure to hear Miss aus der Ohe play the great Tchaikovsky Concerto. The work itself holds its own admirably; very few modern concertos can compare with it in fertility of invention, firmness of musical purpose, and stout construction. There is some rather

unkempt savagery in it, even some triviality now and then; but Tchaikovsky shows in it that he has so much to say, and says it with such force and distinctness that the work cannot but be called admirable . . . It is full of fine fantasy, noble frenzy, haunting melody, and skillful workmanship. Above all, it has a strange, pungent, savage perfume . . . Miss aus der Ohe played it superbly from beginning to end, she was in evident sympathy with the composition, and showed herself at her very best . . . Now, Miss aus der Ohe is a most interesting temperamental study. She glides across the stage, cool, virginal, the Diana of the pianoforte: but the moment she touches the keys she undergoes a transformation; and while she does not lose her self control and while she watches the flight of her musical arrows, little by little she becomes intensely human. Seldom is such virility seen in a woman's playing: and yesterday, her feminine instinct of refinement kept her from abusing her strength. So that while her performance was bold and broad, strong and manly, it was also impassioned; and when occasion required, she showed daintiness, elegance, and sentiment that was never mawkish . . . It was grand playing.[131]

Tchaikovsky had found in aus der Ohe an ideal interpreter of his First Piano Concerto. It was one of his favorite compositions and in his lifetime he conducted this piece more frequently than any of his other works, a total of eleven times; and aus der Ohe performed it with him more than any other pianist, a total of four times.

In November of 1892, Tchaikovsky received a letter from a friend in Vienna telling him of aus der Ohe's recent successes in that city and Tchaikovsky replied, "My dear and great friend! I just received your kind letter. The success of Adele aus der Ohe delights me very much, for she is not only an artist of great talent, but also a very kind and splendid person." He ended the letter with a postscript: "If Miss Adele and her sister are still in Vienna, send them my regards."[132]

In 1893 Tchaikovsky paid aus der Ohe the supreme compliment of inviting her to Russia to play his beloved concerto with him in Saint Petersburg. This performance occurred in October of 1893 in a concert that also featured the premiere of his newly completed Sixth Symphony.[133]

Imperial
Russian Music Society
Saint Petersburg Branch
XXXV Season 1893/94 year

The First Symphonic Session
With the participation of Mme. Aus der Ohe
and the Symphony Orchestra
conducted by P.I. Tchaikovsky
Saturday, October 16, 1893

The Program

1. *The Sixth Symphony in*
   B minor .... *P.I. Tchaikovsky (premiere performance)*
   I. *Adagio*
   II. *Allegro con grazia*
   III. *Allegro molto vivace*
   IV. *Adagio lamentoso*

———

10 minute intermission

———

2. *The overture from an*
   unfinished opera "Carmozina .... *H. Laroche*
   Pianoforte part by **Blumenfeldt** *and* **Lavrov**.

   The plot is based on a comedy of the same name by
   Alfred de Musset

3. *First Concerto in B-flat minor, Op. 23,*
   for piano and orchestra .... *P. Tchaikovsky*
   Performed by **Mme. Aus-der-Ohe**
   I. *Allegro non troppo. Allegro con spirito*
   II. *Andantino. Allegro vivace. Andantino.*
   III. *Allegro con fuoco*

   The concerto was performed for the first time at a
   concert of the Imperial Russian Musical Society in 1875.

4. Dances from the opera "Idomeneo"......................*W. Mozart*
    a) Annonce (Larghetto)
    b) Gavotte

    *The opera was finished and given its first performance
    in Munich in 1781.*

5. Solo for piano. Spanish Rhapsody ....*Liszt*
    Performed by **Mme. Aus-der-Ohe**

Starting at 8:00 p.m.

Aside from the obvious excitement of this concert—
hearing the premiere performance of one of the great symphonies of all time, the Tchaikovsky Sixth, plus one of the
great piano concertos of all time, the Tchaikovsky B-flat
minor, both conducted by the composer himself with his
chosen soloist, the famous Adele aus der Ohe—there are
two notable aspects of this program. The first is that after
the concerto, with only a few minutes of Mozart as separation, aus der Ohe is back on stage to perform Liszt's *Spanish
Rhapsody*. I venture that few pianists would care to return
to the stage to play something as demanding as the *Spanish
Rhapsody* after the huge adrenaline rush and energy output
required of the Tchaikovsky Concerto. She must have been
practically inexhaustible! The second is the inclusion of a
piano solo at all in an orchestral program. It attests to the
great public demand to hear her Liszt performances. It
was inconceivable that this great Liszt interpreter would

ИМПЕРАТОРСКОЕ
РУССКОЕ МУЗЫКАЛЬНОЕ ОБЩЕСТВО
С.-ПЕТЕРБУРГСКОЕ ОТДѢЛЕНІЕ.
XXXV сезонъ, 18⁹³/₉₄ года.

ПЕРВОЕ СИМФОНИЧЕСКОЕ СОБРАНІЕ
ПРИ УЧАСТІИ:
Г-жи Аусъ-деръ-Оэ и оркестра подъ управленіемъ
П. И. Чайковскаго
въ Субботу, 16 Октября 1893 года.

ПРОГРАММА.

1. Шестая симфонія h-moll . . . . . . П. Чайковскаго.
(въ первый разъ).

    I. Adagio.
   II. Allegro con grazia.
  III. Allegro molto vivace.
   IV. Adagio lamentoso.

Антрактъ 10 минутъ.

2. Увертюра къ неоконченной оперѣ
„Кармозина" . . . . Г. Лароша.
Партіи фортепіанно исп. Гг. Блуменфельдъ
и Лавровъ.

Сюжетъ оперы заимствованъ изъ комедіи
того же имени Альфреда де Мюссе. Упер-

Courtesy of Brett Langston of the Tchaikovsky Research Project

тюра написана въ 1869 году. Исполнена
въ первый разъ въ Петербургѣ въ 1872 году,
въ симфоническомъ собраніи Императорскаго
Русскаго Музыкальнаго Общества.

3. Первый концертъ b-moll, op. 23, для
фортепіано съ оркестромъ . . . . . *П. Чайковскаго.*

Исполнитъ Г-жа **Аусъ-деръ-Оэ.**

I. Allegro non troppo. Allegro con
spirito.
II. Andantino. Allegro vivace. Andantino.
III. Allegro con fuoco.

Концертъ исполненъ въ первый разъ
въ симфоническомъ собраніи Императорскаго
Русскаго Музыкальнаго Общества въ 1875 г.

4. Танцы изъ оперы „Идоменей" . . . *В. Моцарта.*
1756—1791

a) Annonce (Larghetto).
b) Gavotte.

Опера окончена и дана въ первый разъ
въ Мюнхенѣ въ 1781 году.

5. Соло для фортепіано. Испанская рап-
содія . . . . *Листа.*

Исполнитъ Г-жа **Аусъ-деръ-Оэ.** 1811—1886.

Начало въ 8 часовъ вечера.

Рояли фабрики Я. БЕККЕРА.

Дирекція СПБ. Отдѣленія покорнѣйше проситъ во время испол-
ненія **не входить и не выходить** изъ залы.

Первое квартетное собраніе состоится въ Субботу, 23 Октября.

Второе симфоническое собраніе состоится въ Субботу, 30 Октября,
подъ управленіемъ Э. Ф. Направника.

Дозволено цензурою. С.-Петербургъ, 14 Октября 1893 г.
Типографія Р. Голике, Спасская улица, № 17.

Рис. 61б. Программа концерта 16 октября 1893 г.
(продолжение)

appear without including at least one piece by Liszt. Every-one wanted to hear this famous student perform her great teacher's music!

Little did anyone know that this concert with aus der Ohe was Tchaikovsky's final one, for shortly afterward he fell ill and within several days was dead. Miss aus der Ohe's touching eyewitness account was published in the *Chicago Daily Tribune*.

It will be recalled that Miss aus der Ohe was the soloist upon the occasion of Tchaikovsky's last public appear-ance in St. Petersburg previous to his death. The frag-mentary and scant account of that event renders Miss aus der Ohe's description of unusual worth.

"Tchaikovsky was well and happy, but there seemed to lurk in his mind the presentiment of sud-den death. In the intermission he spoke of Gounod's demise[134] and of the great age granted him. Several times he repeated, 'If I could only live twenty years more, how much more I could write, what things I might be able to do.' The report that that first per-formance of the Sixth Symphony did not meet with enthusiastic reception was incorrect. The first and last movements were especially well received. Tchaikovsky said with that childlike simplicity that distinguishes him, 'I am so glad they like those movements best; they are my favorites too. The symphony was named during its performance the Pathetique. His Concerto in B-flat minor which I played on this occasion was warmly

received, and I walked up to the conductor's desk and, taking his hand, made him acknowledge the applause which was due to his work, not mine.

The next evening Tchaikovsky invited myself and several friends to dinner. Again the idea of approaching death seemed impressed upon him, although he was apparently in the best of health. He seemed especially anxious to revise his Third Pianoforte Concerto. While the work pleased him he wished to give the solo instrument a greater opportunity. Both that work and his opera Romeo and Juliet, however were doomed never to reach completion.

Tuesday he called upon me and heard me play some of his compositions. Wednesday he should have left for Moscow, where, as I was engaged to play there, I hoped to meet him. For some reason he failed to make his departure.

Thursday he was taken ill, and the disease was pronounced cholera. Notwithstanding the dread with which the disease is held, callers besieged his house, and the physicians, of whom four were in attendance, were obliged to post bulletins on the door to avoid danger of contagion. He remained unconscious for six hours previous to his death, and then, just before his soul fluttered out, he opened his eyes and smiled a last recognition on his brothers.

The whole city of St. Petersburg was in mourning. Crowds viewed the remains and kissed his hand, forgetful of all thoughts of contagion. The funeral was *that of an Emperor. In accordance with the usage of the Greek Church a mass, which was largely attended was held at his house.*

Subsequent ceremonies were held at the cathedral, where some of his most beautiful works were sung, a capella in the Greek style. Admission to the church was only to be obtained through invitation, but outside the streets were blocked by thousands who sadly watched the passage of the procession. The concert given in tribute to his memory was a sad and notable event. His bust, almost covered in flowers and wreaths, was placed in the center of the stage. The audience was clad in somber dress and applause was stifled.

It was difficult to play, I could hardly see the keys for tears.

People felt that a great and noble man was gone and that the hope of musical Russia had found a vast utterance in that Sixth Symphony, which they called his song."

Then, the audience gone and the auditorium in darkness, relieved by a single electric light, Miss aus der Ohe sat down at the piano and played the sad themes of the first and final movement of Tchaikovsky's last symphony; themes penetrating and haunting in their melancholy above anything written by this tone poet of the North, whose death song went out in it.[135]

Falk   949 BROADWAY. N.Y.

MS Mus 132 (9), Houghton Library, Harvard University

Travels

"[Anton] Rubinstein was one of the first European celebrities that ever came to this country. Naturally, when he returned he was asked that ever original question, as to how he had enjoyed the tour, and he replied that the best thing about it was the knowledge that he had made so much money that he would never have to come back."[136]

Rubinstein toured America during the 1872–73 season. He was contracted by Steinway & Sons to play 200 concerts for the unbelievably large fee of $200 per concert. Rubinstein was in America 239 days and during that time played a total of 215 concerts, sometimes playing two or even three in a single day.

Aus der Ohe was behind Rubinstein by only fourteen years. She began her tours in America during the 1886–87 season and very little had changed in the way of the creature comforts of travel. It was still a rather primitive undertaking.

By the mid-1890s, aus der Ohe was in demand everywhere and the touring must have been daunting; but even by their busy standards, Adele and Mathilde's journeys of 1893 and 1894 must surely stand as one of the outstanding feats in the annals of nineteenth century travel.

Aus der Ohe wrote, in February of 1893, from her suite at the Belvedere Hotel in New York City, "A few days ago we returned from Europe..."[137]

She almost immediately headed for the West Coast and while en route played in various cities, including St. Paul, Minnesota. The Schubert Club in St. Paul launched its International Artist Series in 1893 (a series that continues to this day as one of the finest concert series in America). "The ladies of the Schubert Club have undertaken the management of a series of four concerts...The first concert[138] will be held Saturday evening, March 4, with Adele aus der Ohe, the magnificent pianist, as the great attraction..."[139] Thus did the ladies of St. Paul demonstrate their intention of bringing only the very best to Minnesota. The Schubert Club frequently re-engages their artists for second appearances; however, aus der Ohe belongs to a very elite group of only about a dozen artists in the long history of this organization to be invited to make three appearances. She returned to perform for the Schubert Club on January 17, 1895, and again January 28, 1904.

She was in Salt Lake City, Utah on March 7, 1893, and then proceeded on to California where on March 14 she commenced a series of four concerts in San Francisco. She and Mathilde then traveled to Los Angeles and various other southern California cities before returning to San Francisco from where she wrote, "We had a most delightful time here at the Pacific Coast. My last concert is to be

Wednesday next, and after that we start directly for the East, expecting to reach New York during the next week..."[140]

Adele and Mathilde returned to Germany for their annual summer reunion with their brother and sister and in the fall traveled on to Russia.

Her 1894 New Year greeting to her friend, Boston Symphony conductor Wilhelm Gericke, was again posted from the Belvedere Hotel in New York City. She was back where she had been one year earlier:

I spent the first half of this season in Russia—in St Petersburg in the symphony concert of the Imperial Music Association, in Moscow in the Philharmonic concert once again, besides concerts of my own. It was very nice there. In Petersburg I played, still under Tchaikovsky's conducting, his B-flat minor Concerto— ten days before his death. That was his last official appearance! We traveled here at the beginning of the New Year; my first performance was here in the Philharmonic concert under Seidl, on January 12th and 13th. I have commitments until the middle of March, and then we are thinking of returning to Europe.

Allow me still to send you and your dear wife New Year's wishes, which, though late, are heartfelt—it would have been impossible to send them on time due to our sea journey at the end of December...[141]

One is compelled to pause and consider the enormity of these journeys. In January of 1893 they had departed Berlin, by February they were in New York, by March they were already on the West Coast, performing in San Francisco, in April in Los Angeles, then back to San Francisco in May. By early June they were back in New York and then, after their summer vacation in Berlin, by October they were, unbelievably, in St. Petersburg, Russia. Aus der Ohe gave November performances in Moscow and by January of 1894, she and Mathilde were back in New York. Possibly they did not even have time to stop in Berlin as they made their way from Russia, across Europe, and across the Atlantic. And it didn't end there—after side trips to Montreal, Buffalo, etc., they were in Chicago for a February 24, 1894 performance, and then were once more back to Berlin for their annual summer vacation.

These two women, in the span of this single year, 1893, had managed to travel halfway around the earth—from San Francisco, California, to St. Petersburg, Russia! It is amazing that it was possible to accomplish this daunting schedule. Even in our day of fast cars and even faster airplanes, their schedule would be grueling—and we must not forget that the travel was only the means to the end—the necessary evil. The primary task was presenting world-class piano performances night after night to audiences who were expecting near miracles.

As a firm believer in the value of pictures—this, dear reader, is a picture of travel in the nineteenth century.

My friend Jim Reske, a train aficionado from North Carolina, tells me, "This photo illustrates the only useful steam engine designed up to about 1900. The next development was the 4–6–0, i.e., which added a third pair of driving wheels.

"For the time, Campbell's 4–4–0 was a giant among locomotives. Its cylinders measured 14 inch (356 mm) in diameter with a 16 in (406 mm) piston stroke, it boasted 54 in (1.37 m) diameter driving wheels, could maintain 90 lbf/in^2 (620 kPa) of steam pressure and weighed 12 short tons (11 metric tons). Campbell's locomotive was estimated to be able to pull a 450 short ton (410 metric ton) train at 15 mph (24 km/h) on level track, beating the strongest of Baldwin's 4–2–0 s in tractive effort by around 63 percent."[142]

Note the key fact in all this railroad jargon—fifteen miles per hour! Yet despite a capacity of fifteen miles per hour, the average speed was much slower, probably closer to ten or twelve miles per hour. Train speeds were cut into significantly by water and coal stops to keep the engines running, and station stops to let passengers off and on. The Santa Fe railroad even created mealtime stops for their passenger trains in order for passengers to get off the train to eat.

Dining cars did not become common until the late 1890s. Often a rail passenger's option for meal service en route was to patronize one of the roadhouses usually located near the railroad's water stops where "available foods typically consisted of rancid meat, cold beans, and stale coffee."[143]

There was no air conditioning. That did not become a reality until after World War II, even in the United States. The only remedy from summer heat was open windows. In the winter a coal stove was used to heat each car. Steam heat came much later. A problem in the winter was that the coal stove would oftentimes be accidentally upset by passengers and set the train on fire.

Pullman sleeper cars were available in the United States but were expensive. Sleeper cars would also have been available in Europe but probably not in Russia. Some trains had chair cars exclusively and some even had only wooden benches.

Rail travel was noisy and the ride was often not smooth. There was dust and smoke in the air from the coal-burning engines. The toilet facilities were primitive at best. The waste was simply dumped onto the tracks and passengers were requested to refrain from using the toilets while the train was in the station.

And of course, for a pianist, there would have been no access to a piano for practicing on the trains. It is almost mind numbing to think of the interminable hours of monotony and ennui!

Ship travel, by contrast, was quite comfortable and pleasant, perhaps even luxurious—albeit still slow. The average time it took to cross from Bremen, Germany, to New York City was ten days. In contrast to the trains, the food on the ocean crossing steamships was excellent, the air very refreshing, and quite possibly aus der Ohe would even have had access to a piano while aboard the ship, if she wished. The only real unpleasantness was the occasional rough water due to North Atlantic storms.

Some roughly estimated calculations of travel times and distances produce staggering results. The January 1893 Berlin to New York trip was at least eleven days—one day to get from Berlin to Bremen, their usual ship embarkation point, and ten days to cross the ocean; this represents a distance of close to 4,000 miles. Between February 6 and March 14 they traveled from New York to San Francisco, a distance of about 2,500 miles and at an (optimistically) average train speed of fifteen miles per hour, this represents a trip of one week—assuming travel around the clock and with no stops. But of course it was not possible to travel without stops, so we can only guess that the actual amount of time was closer to ten days. Then, of course, once the destinations were reached and once the concerts were completed there was the return—another 2,500 miles (and ten days) to get back to New York and another 4,000 miles and eleven days back to Berlin. That makes for a rough estimate of forty days of continuous travel to get from Berlin to California and back to Berlin.

The distance from Berlin to St. Petersburg, Russia, is more than 800 miles and was a minimum trip of two days' travel each way. Of course, aus der Ohe was playing concerts in many places as she made her way across the United States, and also across Europe and Russia, so the exact number of miles would be far greater, but a conservative estimate is that in this one year, 1893, Adele and Mathilde traveled in excess of 15,000 miles. In 1894 they were back

in New York, from Berlin, and on to Chicago before returning to Berlin for the summer. This represents a minimum
of at least an additional 10,000 miles.

The circumference of the earth at the equator is slightly
more than 24,000 miles. Their mileage (more than 15,000
in 1883 plus more than 10,000 in the first half of 1894) is
greater than the circumference of the earth! It is breath-
taking to think of these two women, in the span of eighteen months accomplishing a distance equivalent to that
of going around the world, doing it all at the rate of about
fifteen miles per hour, and all the while properly attired in
hats and gloves.

We also have to remember that the ships could only go
where there was water and the trains only where there were
tracks. We can (hopefully) assume that each city in which
aus der Ohe appeared was at least on the railroad system—
because the next option was the stagecoach!

And once they arrived at their destination and departed the train station, it was as it had always been—by horse
and buggy, traveling considerably slower than fifteen miles
per hour.

One has to then consider the endless packing and
unpacking as they arrived and departed each city. Women
wore a lot of clothing in those days and many steamer
trunks would have been necessary to transport all this
clothing. Aus der Ohe was traveling as a wealthy celebrity
and she was regularly appearing on stages in front of thousands of people. It was necessary to be dressed elegantly.
Also there were social engagements that required very
different but equally elegant attire. She would have needed

full-length concert gowns, coats and hats, scarves and parasols, shoes and jewelry, petticoats and corsets, etc. And all of this clothing had to be kept clean and crisply starched and ironed.

Occasional miscalculations were made. A letter from New York: "And moreover we have no really warm clothes here as we sent our trunk with them to a friend while we were absent, who is now in Vermont. So what shall we do! We did not expect such winter weather in October as it is here now."[144]

An amusing travel anecdote was related in the *St. Paul Globe*. (The person about whom the story is told, Miss Coons, was a young, talented American pianist studying in Europe at the time.)

During the summer of 1902 she [Miss Coons] and a party composed of her parents, former District Attorney Townes, of New York, and his two daughters were traveling from Geneva to Paris on a railway train.

The afternoon was warm and Miss Townes and Miss Coons had an apartment by themselves. At a way station two women, genteel in appearance and charmingly gowned, entered the carriage. As the journey was long the American girls and the newcomers fell into conversation, which as time went by, drifted upon the topic of palmistry.

"My dear child," said one of the ladies, taking the hand of Miss Coons, "what a wonderful piano player you would make. I never saw a hand so perfect for the piano; every line indicates wonderful love for and

mastery of music. Your fingers, particularly, indicate that you would make one of the greatest players in the world."

"Do you think," asked Miss Townes, "that it is possible for her to become as great as Adele aus der Ohe?"

"I do," replied the stranger emphatically. "This hand indicates that she possesses marvelous ability as well as application, and such a hand never lies."

At this juncture the train halted, and as the two ladies arose to alight the palm reader turned to Miss Coons and said: "I am Adele aus der Ohe. I wish you every success."[145]

Apocryphal? Possibly, but amusing nonetheless; and it would not have been unusual for aus der Ohe to be noticing and commenting on hands. Many pianists have a great curiosity about the structure and size of various hands. Aus der Ohe's own hands were frequently remarked upon: "Under the player's firm white hands—enormous white hands, one is almost tempted to call them for their size is unusual..."[146]

The travel was truly arduous and surely begs the question: Why did she do it? What could possibly have been the motivation behind such frenetic and ceaseless travel?

It is important to remember the times in which she lived, which were so very different from now. We have music in abundance. We can hear music literally everywhere and all the time; it is on our radios and televisions, it is endlessly aired in public buildings, and if all that is not enough one can even carry one's iPod and never be without sound.

But in aus der Ohe's day, none of this existed and, as had been the case since the beginning of time, there were only two ways to hear music: One was to make it yourself, and the other was to listen to someone else make it. Very few people can sit at a piano and play the great classical compositions, so the task fell to the professional performers to bring this great music to the people. Aus der Ohe knew that she had been given extraordinary gifts, and if she did not play, people would not hear—not only would people not hear her, but people would not hear Bach and Beethoven, Chopin and Liszt. I believe she felt a duty, a *"Génie oblige"* to get on those ships and trains, despite every discomfort and inconvenience, and to spread the sound!

And for that her audiences were appropriately appreciative.

Boston Music Hall.

SEASON 1898-99.

BOSTON SYMPHONY ORCHESTRA,

Mr. WILHELM GERICKE, Conductor.

XV. CONCERT.

SATURDAY, FEBRUARY 11, AT 8. P. M.

Programme.

BEETHOVEN.	OVERTURE to " Leonore," No. 3, op. 72.
BRAHMS.	CONCERTO for PIANOFORTE, No. 2, in B-flat major, op. 83. I. Allegro non troppo. II. Allegro appassionato. III. Andante. IV. Allegretto grazioso.
BRUCKNER.	SYMPHONY No. 4, in E-flat major, "Romantic." I. Ruhig bewegt (Allegro molto moderato). II. Andante. III. Scherzo: Bewegt. — Trio: Gemächlich. IV. Finale: Mässig. (First time in Boston).

Soloist:

Miss ADELE AUS DER OHE.

The Pianoforte is a Steinway.

The Music

When I started this book, I worried I would not find enough material to do justice to the life and art of this great lady. I was pleasantly surprised by how much information is available, but it is still, unfortunately, only glimpses into what must have been a wonderfully rewarding and gratifying life. It is in the area of concert programs and repertoire, the great music she played night after night, year after year, where we have perhaps the slightest glimpses of all.

Aus der Ohe began performing publicly at the age of ten, concertized intensely throughout the world during the twenty-year period of 1886–1906, and continued to give concerts in Europe when she was no longer traveling to America. One can conservatively estimate that over the course of her life she gave more than 3,000 concerto, solo, and chamber music performances. The vast majority of these performances are no longer documented. Printed programs were maybe pasted into scrapbooks and cherished for a generation or two but have vanished. In some cases she performed with orchestras that no longer exist and even in halls that no longer exist; and concert notices and reviews were printed in newspapers and magazines that ceased operations decades ago.

However, what remains is, I believe, a fairly representative sampling of aus der Ohe's concert repertoire.[147]

The four cornerstones of her concert programming were Beethoven, Schumann, Chopin, and Liszt. Nearly every recital included a sonata, usually by Beethoven but occasionally by Schumann or Chopin, and every recital concluded with compositions by Liszt. Frequently she also included a grouping of pieces by Chopin. She was a great champion of the music of her day and nearly every recital contained "modern" music. The *Minneapolis Journal* commented, "The tendency of pianists to play the same old time-worn favorites is the occasion of frequent comment and Miss aus der Ohe, who habitually interprets new and unfamiliar works, is to be commended for her courage in leaving the well beaten path."[148]

Music criticism is itself an art and has always been an important aspect of the performing arts. One of the finest practitioners of this art of musical criticism was Boston critic Philip Hale (1854–1934). He was himself a musician and his writings were widely read and highly respected. In addition to his newspaper work, he also wrote program notes for the Boston Symphony. It is from Mr. Hale that we get a sense of aus der Ohe being somewhat ahead of her time, especially in her Beethoven interpretations, in eschewing the romantic excesses that were prevalent in her day.

*I do not know whether she did or did not play the Wald-
stein Sonata in the "true spirit" of Beethoven, for I have
never been able to find out what the "true spirit" exactly
is. Neither Beethoven nor any one of his contemporaries, nor any one of his pupils has given us definite
information. If a pianist should play this Sonata as
though it were a piece by Chopin, he would surely be
open to censure, for the styles of the two men are radi-
cally different; and so when Paderewski plays music
by Beethoven it seldom gives pleasure to the thoughtful,
for his peculiar romanticism does not exhibit Beethoven in his peculiar strength and beauty. Beethoven,
of all composers, laughs at a poseur... Miss aus der
Ohe yesterday was at her very best and her best is not
easily excelled... In supreme moments yesterday she
swept everything before her, and there was no thought
of comparison with other pianists, in certain ways
she is inimitable. And, remember, that her great and
noble qualities make you forget the absence of purely
sensuous charm in tone. After all, sensuousness is not
the final word in music.*[149]

*"The Sonata [Beethoven's Appassionata Op. 57] was
played with a reverence that was not fetishism, with
chaste beauty of tone, with passion that was never
extravagant...*[150] *She is not a warm colorist; she finds
pleasure chiefly in contrasts of black and white. She
does not mix colors deftly with the pedals... She is not
distinguished by caressing warmth of tone... She has*

been called cool, if not cold. The charge is unjust; but
her passion is that of Diana[151] *rejoicing in the sureness*
of her aim, not of Venus smiling with her cestus . . .[152] *As*
she is today, she is unique . . . I know of no woman who
is today her rival, unless it be Theresa Carreño."[153]

The music of Robert Schumann was very important to
aus der Ohe and it was a rare program that did not include
Schumann's music. In addition to the Concerto, she performed most of his greatest piano solo masterpieces,
including *Papillons*, *Carnaval*, the Fantasy Pieces of Op. 12,
the *Symphonic Etudes*, the C major Fantasy that Schumann
had dedicated to Liszt, *Faschingsschwank aus Wien* (Carnival Scenes from Vienna), and the G minor Sonata. She
also performed both the Piano Quartet, Op. 47 and the
Piano Quintet, Op. 44. Her Schumann performances were
always highly praised. Regarding her interpretation of the
G minor Sonata, Philip Hale had this to say:

It is hard to say in which field of piano-playing Miss
aus der Ohe excelled. Had a stranger to her left after
the Sonata, he might have doubted her ability to play
the Polonaise of Liszt with such dazzling brilliance; or
hearing only this Polonaise he might have questioned the
power to interpret Schumann in his most intimate mood.

An ingenious Frenchman, Jean Hubert, has written
an elaborate study of Schumann's G minor Sonata. He
describes the daily and the musical life of the composer
during the five years that he took in writing it, quotes
the objections made to the work, refutes them to his own

satisfaction, lugs in an account of the three women that influenced Schumann, and then gives an exhaustive and exhausting analysis of the Sonata. I have read this book; I have heard others play the Sonata; but I first recognized its strength and beauty last night. For the performance was remarkable in presentation of the text and in suggested commentary. Schumann's music was played in Schumannesque spirit, as though the composer himself spoke through the medium of the pianist. [154]

An extremely interesting comment concerning Schumann's *Carnaval* appeared in a review from the *London Times*. Schumann's *Carnaval* Op. 9 is, in addition to being one of his greatest and most beloved works, also one of his happiest. It is a set of twenty-one character pieces. Each has a title and represents a character you might meet at a carnival, such as a clown, a friend, and even an old girlfriend! Between the eighth and ninth pieces, however, lies one of the great mysteries of the piano repertoire: *Sphinxes*. They are a total of eleven notes, divided into three segments written in almost medieval notation, and they represent the themes from which the entire piece is built. Although theories abound, no one really knows what to do with these. Should they be played or not (most think not)? If they are played are they loud or soft, slow or fast, legato or staccato? And if you don't play them do you sit quietly for a few moments to observe a silence, or do you simply ignore them all together? The *London Times* reported, "Mlle. aus der Ohe ... in Schumann's *Carnaval* (played, by the way, with the *Sphinxes* included) ..." [155] Hmmm—interesting. We know she played *Carnaval* in Liszt's Master Classes and she was a friend of Clara Schumann—maybe she knew a thing or two about those bewildering *Sphinxes*!

She played a great deal of Chopin, including many of his etudes, waltzes, and nocturnes, both the G minor and A-flat Ballades, the *Andante Spianato and Grand Polonaise*, the A-flat Polonaise, the *Berceuse* and the B-flat minor Sonata Op. 35. Aus der Ohe's interpretations of Chopin were lauded nearly as highly as her Liszt. "A great pianist is Adele aus der Ohe. Had she played nothing last night...but the Chopin B-flat minor Sonata and the Liszt *Tarantella di Bravura*, she would have demonstrated her right to the adjective...Miss aus der Ohe's interpretation of each was masterly."[156]

Her Liszt repertoire was very large. She played his etudes, including the D-flat *Un sospiro*, *Waldesrauschen* and *Gnomenreigen*, and *Eroica*, *Ricordanza*, and the F minor from the *Transcendental Etudes*. She played his Hungarian Rhapsodies including numbers 2, 9, and 12, and the *Spanish Rhapsody*; she played waltzes, including the Second and Third *Mephisto Waltzes* and the *Valse Oubliée*. She played the Tarantella from the Italian Pilgrimages (*Années de pèlerinage*–Book 2) and the Polonaise. She frequently included Liszt's transcriptions as well. Her performances of the *Don Juan Fantasy* from Mozart's opera *Don Giovanni* were famous. She played many of Liszt's Wagner opera transcriptions as well as Bach-Liszt, Chopin-Liszt, Schubert-Liszt, etc. She played both Concertos as well as the Hungarian Fantasy for Piano and Orchestra. Her performances of Liszt's music, and especially his E-flat Concerto, were legendary. "In the interpretation of Liszt it may be said of her that in the subjugation of technique to higher musical sense, Miss aus der Ohe is seldom, and even then remotely, approached..."[157] After a performance in Bayreuth, Germany, which included Liszt's *Spanish Rhapsody*, Cosima Wagner, the daughter of Liszt, declared, "She has an extraordinary gift; she has just the spirit of my father, which is rare to find."[158]

The famous nineteenth century Viennese piano pedagogue, Theodor Leschetizky (1830–1915), "who knows genius when he finds it, paid a high tribute to her versatility as a player when he said, 'everything blossoms under your hands.' Beethoven, Schumann, Chopin, Brahms, Liszt, and Tchaikovsky find in her a faithful, willing medium. It is aus der Ohe to be sure, but you recognize the leonic strength of Beethoven, the butterflies, the bloom, and the delicate aroma of Chopin, the romanticism of Schumann, the brilliancy and fire of Liszt, and the wild passion of Tchaikovsky."[159]

Of Bach, she, of course, played the obligatory transcriptions that were demanded of every performing pianist of the day, but she also played his original compositions, including the *Italian* Concerto, the C minor Fantasy, the G minor English Suite, the G major French Suite, and the *Chromatic Fantasy and Fugue*. Very few pianists at that time played this much "untranscribed" Bach.

She programmed early composers such as Couperin, Rameau, and Scarlatti. These composers were not often played and they lent additional interest to aus der Ohe's recitals.

Schubert's music also frequently appeared on her recital programs. In addition to several of the Schubert-Liszt song transcriptions, she often performed an impromptu or selections from *Moment Musicaux*. She was noted for her interpretation of Schubert's great *Wanderer Fantasy* in C major and this piece was often included in recital programs.

In her early years she played the Wilhelm Taubert Concerto No. 1 Op. 18.[160] This work is now virtually unknown.

Over the course of her career, she performed various compositions that were dedicated to her. One of these was the gargantuan Concerto in E minor by Max Vogrich. Vogrich was an Austrian pianist and composer born in 1852. In the 1870s he performed across Europe and it is possible he might have known aus der Ohe from her student days in Germany. He subsequently moved to America where he certainly would have been acquainted with aus der Ohe's artistry. Vogrich is chiefly remembered as a music editor but he composed a substantial number of works during his life, including the Piano Concerto that he dedicated to aus der Ohe and that she premiered with the Boston Symphony on February 9, 1889.[161]

The performance itself was highly praised. "Miss Adele aus der Ohe...has never won a more pronounced triumph here than on this occasion...Few such achievements as that of this artist in her last evening's performance have been known in the history of pianoforte playing in Boston..."[162]

The composition, however, didn't fare quite so well. "The concerto has fitly been called a 'colossal work'...such a torrent of difficulties that the average mind fails to grasp the idea of the composer, and is simply dazed by the stupendous task it presents to the player...it is a trying series of splendid finger-fireworks, needing the greatest skill in technique to overcome and to perform, and when it is all done, not worth the trouble taken with it as far as the purely musical aspect of the work is concerned ... Miss aus der Ohe played it with tremendous energy, and overcame its difficulties in the most brilliant manner ... Whether it was worth doing is quite another question, but it was done, and with the most exciting effect. The artist was recalled four times with as wild an enthusiasm as has ever been manifested at these concerts."[163]

One of the few students of Paderewski, the Polish composer and pianist Sigismund Stojowski (1870–1946), dedicated a Ballade to aus der Ohe.

The American composer Arthur Foote (1853–1937), who was born in Salem, Massachusetts, and lived his entire life in the Boston area, dedicated one of his most substantial piano compositions, "Five poems after Omar Khayyam" Op. 41, to her.

Another American, Henry Holden Huss (1862–1953), was a lifelong resident of New York and considered by many to be one of the finest composers of his generation. He dedicated two compositions to aus der Ohe; a short piano piece entitled "Prelude Appassionata" Op. 7 No. 1, and his Piano Concerto in B major Op. 10. Aus der Ohe performed both of these works.

The Huss concerto[164] is unique in one interesting feature—it was the first piano concerto ever composed in the key of B major. Aus der Ohe liked it—she took it on one of her German tours and then on November 14, 1903, performed it in America with the Boston Symphony.

The critics noted, "...a composition well suited to her style and temperament...It is the work of a young writer, eager to speak out what is on his mind, and not pausing too long to argue or elaborate. The nominal key is the bold, brilliant and exciting B major, and the casting is into the usual three movements. The themes are short and strongly set out, and the regulation cadenza is placed near the middle of the first movement, instead of being held back until time for the coda to be shaped...Many of the themes are strikingly beautiful, others are stirring; there are moments of lovely orchestration...Miss aus der Ohe...aroused great enthusiasm by her noble playing...the artist was recalled four or five times and received some huge floral tributes."[165]

Aus der Ohe performed the Huss Concerto on tour with the Boston Symphony in a total of five cities, including Philadelphia on December 9 and concluding on December 11 in Brooklyn. The great French pianist Raoul Pugno (1852–1914) took a liking to the concerto and requested of Mr. Huss the privilege of performing it in France, which occurred December 18, 1904, with Gabriel Pierné (1863–1937) conducting.

Sometimes aus der Ohe programmed works of composers she might have known from her student days, such as Carl Tausig and Juliusz Zarebski.

Carl Tausig (1841–1871), like aus der Ohe, began his studies with Liszt as a child, at the age of fourteen, and quickly became a favorite of Liszt's. He was a brilliant pianist and many predicted a great future for him, but tragically he died from typhoid fever in 1871 at the age of twenty-nine. Aus der Ohe was only ten years old at the time of his death, so it is unlikely she knew him or ever heard him play—unlikely, but not impossible. The Ohe family was living in Berlin by 1870 and Tausig was performing throughout Europe up to the time of his death, so perhaps as a young child she did hear Tausig play and perhaps he had made quite a profound impression on her. Or perhaps she simply heard stories of him from Liszt and wished to honor this great pianist who died such an untimely death. In any case, aus der Ohe clearly had a deep respect for him, for throughout her career she often inserted a Tausig composition into her recital programs.

Juliusz Zarebski (1854–1885), whose name is frequently misspelled as Zarembski (for this is how it is pronounced in Polish), was a student of Liszt from 1874 to 1877, the very years when aus der Ohe was beginning her youthful work with the great master, so aus der Ohe certainly would have known him. Early in her career she performed various Zarebski compositions including his Grand Polonaise Op. 6. His music was highly praised by Liszt, who said, "Naturally, Chopin is incomparable, but since Chopin, I know no one who has hit upon the Polish character with such art and nobility as Zarebski."[166]

In the unfortunate realm of might-have-been performances, we read this from a Boston newspaper of 1897.

Mme. Eames[167] was announced for this concert, but sudden indisposition prevented her coming on from New York, and Miss aus der Ohe was induced to exchange dates with her at short notice. Besides our being heartily sorry to hear of Mme. Eames illness, we

could not but feel an added pang of regret at one result
of this sudden change. Miss aus der Ohe was to have
appeared at the symphony concerts here consider-
ably later in the season, and intended to play the new
pianoforte concerto by Eugene d'Albert. But she was
not ready to play it at such short notice, so she chose
Liszt's in E-flat instead. We have thus lost the d'Albert
Concerto for this season at least.[168]

It appears the loss was permanent, for there is no subsequent documentation of an aus der Ohe performance of
the d'Albert Concerto.

Aus der Ohe was so famous for her large repertoire
that readers would have understood and appreciated the
humor of an article that appeared in *The Music Trade Review*
in 1900. The article, entitled "The Piano Salesman," is
quite long and makes it abundantly clear that to be a piano
salesman is no slight undertaking! "The successful piano
salesman must be an artist...must needs be a Talleyrand
or a Richelieu for diplomacy and a Demosthenes for elo-
quence...he must be a good performer with a repertoire
at his fingertips that would startle Adele aus der Ohe..."[169]

Aus der Ohe's wide repertoire allowed her to give her
audiences broad views of the piano literature. Already
within a year of her American debut she played both Liszt
concertos two nights apart, showing the various aspects of
Liszt's concerto writing. In 1903 she played Tchaikovsky's
Concerto No. 2 in G major and then only about a week later
his No. 1 in B-flat minor, again showing a larger picture of
Tchaikovsky than one would have hearing only one con-

certo. When she appeared in the larger cities of America and Europe, aus der Ohe typically played two solo recitals rather than only one, giving her audiences a wider exposure to the repertoire as well as a larger sense of her interpretive abilities.

She presented one of her typical two-recital series in 1891 in Philadelphia at the Academy of Music. The first program occurred on February 19, and the second on February 21, a mere forty-eight hours later.

These two programs were repeated one month later in Boston, on the fourteenth and the sixteenth of March— again played only two days apart. These programs contain an unusually large amount of very difficult music. Of special interest is the predominance of C major—is this by design or coincidence? The two Beethoven sonatas are his largest piano compositions in C major, the *Wanderer Fantasy*, in C major, is one of Schubert's most ambitious piano works, and, similarly, the Schumann Fantasy is one of Schumann's largest piano compositions and is too in C major. It is almost as if aus der Ohe is presenting a study of the possibilities of the key of C.

On February 9 and 16, 1897, at Steinert Hall in Boston, she played two very large recital programs, this time a week apart.

Adele aus der Ohe had a lifelong commitment to chamber music. As early as 1883 when she was but twenty-two years old and still a student at Weimar, *The Monthly Musical Record* reported, "As far as I know she is the first pianist who plays, not only her large repertoire of solo pieces, but also the most complicated ensemble music, classical and

FIRST RECITAL, THURSDAY EVENING, FEBRUARY 19th.

Programme

✳   ✳   ✳   ✳   ✳   ✳

1. **Sonate,** *C major, op. 2, No.* 3, ...   BEETHOVEN

  Allegro con brio.
    Adagio.
      Scherzo.
        Allegro assai.

2. a. **Passepieds,** .   .   .   .   VOGRICH

  b. **Presto,** *E major, op.* 7, *No.* 7, ...   MENDELSSOHN

  c. **Nocturne,** *D flat, op.* 27, *No.* 2, ...   CHOPIN

  d. **Valse,** *Caprice,* .   .   .   .   TAUSIG

3. **Fantasie,** *C major, op.* 15, ...   SCHUBERT

  Allegro con brio ma non troppo.
    Adagio (Der Wanderer.)
      Presto.
        Allegro.

4. a. **Etude de Concert,** *D flat,* .   .   .   .   ⎫
                                                      ⎬   LISZT
  b. **Grand Polonaise,** .   .   .   .   .   .   ⎭

Music Division, The New York Public Library for the Performing Arts, The New York Public Library, Astor, Lenox and Tilden Foundations

Second Recital, Saturday Afternoon, February 21st, at 3 o'clock.

Programme

1. **Sonate,** *C major, op.* 53, ... BEETHOVEN

      Allegro con brio.
         Introduzione (Adagio molto.)
            Allegretto moderato. Prestissimo.

2. a. **Gavotte,** *D minor* (From Suites Anglaises), ... BACH

  b. **Valse,** . . . . ⎫
  c. **Nocturne,** *B major, op.* 9, *No.* 3, ... ⎬ CHOPIN
  d. **Polonaise,** *A flat, op.* 53, ... ⎭

3. **Fantasie,** *C major, op.* 17, ... SCHUMANN
              (Dedicated to Franz Liszt.)

   I. *Durchaus phantastisch und leidenschaftlich vorzutragen.*
     Im Legenden Ton. Erstes Tempo.

  II. *Maessig. Durchaus energisch. Etwas langsamer. Viel bewegter.*

 III. *Langsam getragen. Durchweg leise zu halten.*

SCHUMANN'S FANTASIE, op. 17, composed in 1836, was to have been published for the
benefit of the fund for the Beethoven Monument, to be erected at Bonn. On the title page was to
be printed "Obolus," and the three movements were respectively called "Ruins," "Triumphant
Arch," "Starry Crown." Afterwards Schumann gave up this idea and the titles were replaced by
the following motto from Fr. Schlegel, very characteristic of a Fantasie by Schumann.

             "Mid all the chords that vibrate through"
             "Earth's strangely checkered dream,"
             "There runs a note whose gentle tone"
             "Is heard aright by him alone"
             "Who lists with care extreme."

  "The Fantasy" he writes to his betrothed, "thou canst understand only by going back to the
unhappy Summer of 1836, when I gave thee up," and in another letter he says:—"Write me what
thou thinkest to thyself during the first movement; does it not call up many images to thee? Art
thou indeed 'the tone' in the motto? I almost believe so."
  This Fantasy with its transporting poetic flights, its wealth of deeply tender, fervent and powerful thoughts so richly orchestrally dressed, is one of Schumann's most beautiful works.

4. **Don Juan Fantasie,** . . . . LISZT

TUESDAY AFTERNOON, FEBRUARY 9, AT 2.30

. . PROGRAM . .

1. *a.* Toccata and Fugue, D minor,   .   .   .   *Bach–Tausig*

    b. Suite Anglaise, G minor, ...   *Bach*
            Prelude, Sarabande, Gavotte, Gigue.

    c. Sonata, F minor, Op. 57, ...   *Beethoven*
            Allegro assai. Andante con moto.
            Allegro ma non troppo. Presto.

2. *a.* Die heiligen drei Brunnen bei Trafoi (The Sacred
        Three Springs near Trafoi), .   .   .   *Franz Kullak*

    b. Prelude and Fugue, D minor, Op. 15,   .   *Arthur Foote*

    c. Three Études, Op. 25, Nos. 1, 2, and 3,
    d. Valse, A-flat, Op. 42, ...   *Chopin*
    e. Andante and Polonaise,   .   .

3. *a.* Barcarole, F minor, ...   *Rubinstein*

    b. Étude, ...   *Adèle Aus der Ohe*

    c. Rhapsodie Hongroise, No. 12, ...   *Liszt*

Steinway Pianos used exclusively by Miss Aus der Ohe.

Music Division, The New York Public Library for the Performing Arts, The New York Public Library, Astor, Lenox and Tilden Foundations

TUESDAY AFTERNOON, FEBRUARY 16, AT 2.30

. . PROGRAM . .

1. Sonate, C major, Op. 53, ... *Beethoven*
Allegro con brio.
Molto Adagio.
Allegretto, Moderato, Prestissimo.

2. *a.* Variations Sérieuses, ...
    b. Two Songs without Words : . .   } . *Mendelssohn*
       No. 1, F major ; No. 2, Spinning Song,

    c. Presto, Op. 7, ...

    d. Chromatic Fantasy and Fugue, ... *Bach*
          (Bülow Edition.)

    e. Berceuse, ... *Chopin*

    f. Valse Caprice, ... *Tausig*

3. *a.* Suite, Op. 2, ... *Adèle Aus der Ohe*
       Bourée. Sarabande. Menuet. Gavotte.

    b. Nocturne, No. 1, ... } . . . *Liszt*
    c. Tarantelle from Venezia e Napoli,

Steinway Pianos used exclusively by Miss Aus der Ohe.

modern, without book. I confess that this gift adds essentially to one's pleasure in listening to the talented artist. If it is generally acknowledged that it is useful, and almost necessary, for a virtuoso to play solos by heart, why should it not be also an advantage for the performance of chamber music?"[170]

In an 1887 letter in which she discussed possible concert dates in Newark, New Jersey, aus der Ohe commented: "As I like very much to play chamber music..."[171]

In America she appeared frequently with the Kneisel Quartet which had been founded by Franz Kneisel, concert master of the Boston Symphony.

In Miss Adele aus der Ohe, Mr. Kneisel has obtained an ensemble player who though a virtuoso, is able and willing to join her artistic individuality with that of her companions in the performance of the music she undertakes, and to be but one factor with them in its interpretation. She evidently views the task of an ensemble player very seriously and she played her part in Schumann's piano quartet from memory—a procedure that has its disadvantages as well as its advantages, but that certainly results in a greater freedom and flexibility.

The performance of the entrancing music—music of Schumann's most poetic and intimate inspiration— was one of the most delightful pieces of ensemble playing that could be imagined. Miss aus der Ohe's tone joined beautifully with those of the strings, and it was colored and varied in quality and subtly adjusted in its proportions to the proper effect of the whole.

The quartet was played with joyous and elastic
spirit, with the true lyric note that ought to dominate
it, with flashing brilliancy in the scherzo, and with
warmth and poetic charm in the andante...[172]

Frequently she programmed her own music. Composing was a very important aspect of aus der Ohe's life and she composed always, from the time she was a young student until nearly the end of her life. Her letters often speak of her composition work.

In 1897: "At present we are here [in Berlin] and I am very busy with my music, studying and writing a great deal."[173]

A letter to Mrs. Gilder in 1898: "I have written a great deal of music of late and should wish I could play it to you soon."[174]

In 1901: "I have been very busy playing and writing. Some new piano pieces are now again published by Mr. G. Schirmer in New York. I played a group of my things in Berlin before leaving, and was pleased that they were liked."[175]

In 1905: "I would need a room where I could have my grand piano and where I could practice and work undisturbed some hours each day . . . we wish to stay for a longer time and I want a great deal of time for my work."[176]

And in 1909: "I have been very very busy with my art."[177]

An article entitled "Women Composers" appeared in the March 1898 issue of *The Century Magazine*. Aus der Ohe commented in a letter to Mrs. Gilder, "I was so pleased to read the article about Women Composers in the March *Century*."[178]

"Germany is well represented by the compositions of Fräulein aus der Ohe. Her preeminence as a pianist has left her little time for composition; but the quality of what she has done is very high. Fräulein aus der Ohe's compositions possess the substantial and vigorous qualities of her playing."[179]

Aus der Ohe's compositions can be divided into three genres: vocal solos, piano solos, and violin and piano music. The songs for voice and piano, a total of thirteen songs that are divided among four Opus numbers, were all written early in her career. Aus der Ohe's first Opus is a set of four songs for voice and piano that were published in New York in 1895 by G. Schirmer. The texts for these songs are from a book of poetry entitled *The New Day* by her friend Richard Watson Gilder. The four songs are: "The Birds Were Singing"; "A Birthday Song," "with a beautiful figure repeated in the accompaniment; and a fluty bird lyric"[180]; "Not From the Whole Wide World," which "has a somberness of treatment that gives its love-message a religious fervor; its postlude is happily given to a voice that seems to answer the song";[181] and the last is "Thistledown," which, "save for a dramatic moment, has all the airiness of its subject."[182]

Opuses 5, 6, and 7 are also all songs. Opus 5 consists of a set of five songs set to poems of Richard Gilder: "Rose-Dark the Solemn Sunset," "After Sorrow's Night," "Cradle Song," "I Care Not if the Skies are White," which has "a striking vocal skip of a tenth,"[183] and "Winds to the Silent Morn."

Opus 6 consists of two songs: "The Orphans" with text by Adalbert Chamisso[184] "in which the plaint of an orphan is brought to a wild climax";[185] and "I Grieve to See These Tears," "which has a bitter pathos and a wailing refrain with a guitar style accompaniment."[186] The text for this song as well as the Opus 7 set was by her friend Robert Underwood Johnson.[187]

The two songs that make up Opus 7 are "I Begged a Kiss of a Little Maid" and "Some Said They Did But Play At War."

Nothing is known of any of aus der Ohe's songs beyond the fact that they exist. Aus der Ohe never mentioned performances of any songs in any of her correspondence, and there are no known newspaper articles or programs indicating any song performances. All are scored for high voice, either soprano or tenor, and it is not known if she had a particular singer in mind. Of course they are all long out of print; however, a selection of six songs was republished in 1985 by Recital Publications in Huntsville, Texas. They are lovely works.

Aus der Ohe frequently performed her piano solo compositions, and they were always well received by both the critics and the audience.

Her Suite for Pianoforte Op. 2 "has made a deep impression upon severe critics, and indeed is a real achievement. Written in the old style, it is remarkable for catching the very spirit of that music. It is not a mere happy imitation, but an expression so spontaneous and personal that Bach himself might have been proud of it. Here is pure music that is at the same time full of life. Even better than the sturdy gaiety of the Bourée, the stateliness of the Sarabande, or the crystalline cheeriness of the Minuet, is the Gavotte, contrasting as it does the hauteur of the principal movement with the sprightliness of the Musette."[188]

Opus 3 is an *Etude de Concert*, "highly praised by Tchaikovsky. It is an ideal bravura study, because its great technical difficulties do not seem to be dragged in for their own sake, but rather to be caught up and swept along in one tempestuous idea. It is also published in a simplified edition."[189] Both the Suite Op. 2 and the Concert Etude were published in New York by G. Schirmer in 1895.

In 1897 Schirmer published her Opuses 4, 5, 6, and 7. Opus 4 is a set of three piano pieces entitled Melody in F, "Slumber Song," and "Rustic Dance (Bauerntanz)," "which is rather programmatic; it opens somewhat like that other peasant festival, Grieg's 'Wedding March,' with a thumping of stout fifths; a rollicking, boisterous dance ensues, followed by a moment of regretful farewell; then with a dash it is all over."[190]

At the beginning of her career she often included one or two of her pieces either as part of her printed program or as an encore, but around 1898 her compositions began to occupy more substantial portions of her recital programs. She performed for the first time her newly published Suite Op. 8 in New York at a November 22, 1898 recital.

Miss aus der Ohe's name will have to be added to the role of female composers. She has not yet displayed creative power, but her faculty of assimilation is highly developed, and what she produces bears the unmistakable stamp of her own individuality. This was noticeably the excellence of the suite heard yesterday for the first time. Its movements are a Prelude, a Sarabande, an À la Bourée, an Air, a Gavotte, and a Gigue. The style and techniques of the composition are the product of Miss aus der Ohe's thorough absorption of the works of Bach and their modern arrangement by Tausig and others. Her musical ideas and her development of them were in imitation, and very successful and musicianly imitation, of the antique style, while the pianistic embroidery in which the whole was garbed was modern in its details. The composition as a whole is an uncommonly scholarly piece of work, and in thought, feeling, and form more austere in tone than one would expect from a woman.

The Air in particular, displays a remarkable continence in musical diction, and a striking freedom from easy sentimentality. The Prelude is well made, very clear in its polyphony, and withal rhythmic and bright. The Bourée movement is admirable in its frank humor and general atmosphere of gayety. The Gigue deserves special mention for its perfect character. It is a genuine gigue, with just a suspicion of Celticism in its melodic sequences. The suite, as a whole, should find its way into the repertoires of all pianists who are not troubled with envy and small professional jealousy.[191]

Musical America noted, "She surprised everybody as a composer...it is not the excellent workmanship as shown in this Suite that does the most credit to Miss aus der Ohe, for workmanship can be acquired by others. No, the distinguishing feature is her genuine gift of invention. There is a freshness about her themes and a spontaneity in the way she develops them, both of which are thoroughly fascinating; and above all, there is unmistakable individuality behind aus der Ohe, the composer. The Suite made a hit with the audience."[192]

The Commercial Advertiser exclaimed, "Miss aus der Ohe is to be congratulated on her achievement, for she has made a valuable addition to the music for pianoforte."[193]

The Sun enthused, "...it proved a genuine artistic triumph for its inventor."[194]

The Opus 8 Suite and a set of four pieces, Opus 9, were both published in Berlin by Ries and Erler in 1901. The Four Pieces Opus 9 are entitled: *Eine Sage (A Legend)*, *Walzer*, *Novellette*, and *Spinnlied (Spinning Song)*. This last work is fashioned after Mendelssohn's famous *Spinning Song* and aus der Ohe frequently performed both hers and Mendelssohn's in concert.

In 1902 G. Schirmer of New York published aus der Ohe's Opuses 10 and 11. Opus 10 is two piano solos, *Melodie* and *Berceuse*, and Opus 11 is a Mazurka for piano solo.

Aus der Ohe undoubtedly had Liszt's Villa d'Este tribute *Les Jeux d'eau à la Villa d'Este (The Fountains of the Villa d'Este)* in mind as she composed her own tribute to this remarkable place. Op. 13 is a Concert Etude entitled *Am Springbrunnen— Eine Erinnerung an Villa d'Este (By the Fountain—A Remembrance of the Villa d'Este)* and was published in 1906 in New York, again by G. Schirmer, as were also Opus 14, and Opus 16. This Concert Etude bears the inscription *Meiner Schwester Mathilde gewidmet* (Dedicated to my sister Mathilde).

In the later years of his life, Liszt spent part of each winter as a house guest at the Villa d'Este, in Tivoli, just outside of Rome. Aus der Ohe had studied there with Liszt as early as 1875, while still in her teen years. Quite possibly she and Mathilde had even lodged at the Villa during these times of Adele's work with Liszt. It is intoxicating to think of the lovely remembrances Adele and Mathilde must have had of their time at the Villa; evenings of conversation and music with Liszt in this magnificent seventeenth century Renaissance palace set amid magnificent gardens and water fountains!

Opus 14 consists of five pieces for solo piano: *Morgenliedchen (Morning Song), Pastorale, Walzer, Lustiges Intermezzo (Merry Interlude),* and *Am Sommerabend (On a Summer Evening).*

A tantalizing might-have-been was reported in 1904—first in *The Music Trade Review:* "A new Piano Concerto by Miss aus der Ohe is to have its first public performance in Berlin in October."[195] And then in the *New York Times:* "Adele aus der Ohe returned from Europe on Tuesday last and will make her first appearance this winter in Carnegie Hall on December 15 and 16. While abroad Miss aus der Ohe arranged for the publication of her new Concerto for Piano and Orchestra . . . It is possible that the concerto will have its first performance at the Philharmonic concert."[196] Unfortunately the Philharmonic concert featured the Liszt E-flat Concerto and nothing more is known of this piano concerto. It appears to have been intended as her Opus 15 but was, for unknown reasons, withdrawn. It would be fascinating to have aus der Ohe's thoughts on how a piano concerto ought to be written—she had performed so many by other composers. A disappointing loss.

Two of aus der Ohe's published opus numbers are works for piano and violin. The first, Three Pieces for Violin and Piano Op. 12, was published in 1903 in New York by G. Schirmer. The three pieces are *Mazurka, Romanze,* and *Die Elfe tanzt (Dancing Elf).*

Aus der Ohe's final published composition is a Sonata

for Violin and Piano in F-sharp Op. 16. The premiere of this sonata occurred in Boston on January 2, 1905, with Mr. Will Hess, concertmaster of the Boston Symphony, at a concert of the Boston Symphony Quartet. A Boston critic noted, "It would hardly be possible to over praise the beauty of this poetic conception."[197] A week later, on January 9, she and Mr. David Mannes played it in New York. David Mannes was a prominent American violinist who, along with his wife Clara Damrosch, would eventually found one of the finest music conservatories in America, the Mannes School of Music in New York City. The New York critics were, unfortunately, less impressed with the piece, noting, "The sonata, of course, discloses the hand of one who can write effectively for the instrument, but it also seems to show an uncertainty in maintaining the longer flight and sustained power that are needed to achieve a sonata."[198]

Aus der Ohe was a relatively prolific composer despite the rigors of her performing career. By 1906 her published compositions totaled nearly forty pieces. Of course all of these are long, long out of print; however, copies of some of these compositions can be obtained from the Library of Congress in America and from the State Library in Berlin.

She continued to compose throughout her final decades in Berlin; however, none of her music written after 1906 was published. In Hamburg in 1910 she performed a Suite in B minor that was highly praised. Except for this Suite, we know nothing about her work after 1906. Her letters indicate that she was always busily working but say nothing of what she was working on.

For nearly her entire life she had been constantly on

the move—ship travel across the Ocean, train travel from city to city all across America and Europe and even Russia, always living out of hotels—and of course practicing always had to be the first priority.

Once these demanding years of travel and concertizing were over, the opportunity to spend long afternoons of solitude in the comfort of her own home for the quiet, uninterrupted work that composing requires must have been a real joy for aus der Ohe.

Of her manuscripts, sadly, nothing has survived—not even the manuscripts of her published compositions—except for a very few tiny scraps of music such as the one reproduced here, which was preserved by her friends, the Gilders. Possibly this fragment was intended to be included in some publication, or perhaps it was simply given in remembrance of the great friendship aus der Ohe shared with Mr. and Mrs. Gilder. It is the final bars of her Op. 13, *Am Springbrunnen—Eine Erinnerung an Villa d'Este (By the Fountain—A Remembrance of the Villa d'Este)* and is as beautiful for the eye as it is for the ear, a true work of art.

Courtesy The Lilly Library, Indiana University, Bloomington, Indiana

Etude de Concert.

Allegro con spirito.

ADELE AUS DER OHE.
Op. 3.

Piano.

MATHILDE AUS DER OHE

(An enlargement from Louis Held's 1883 photo
outside the Hofgärtnerei)

Mathilde

By the second half of the 1890s, aus der Ohe's American career and reputation were solidly established. She continued to tour in America every season but she also began to focus on her European career. European engagements meant less time traveling and more time at home. Around 1896 or 1897, she and Mathilde moved from the family home in Zehlendorf into an elegant apartment at Ansbacherstrasse 7 in the fashionable Western section of Berlin. This home combined the convenience of city life with the natural beauty of the quite nearby Tiergarten. From this 1893 description, one can easily see why aus der Ohe would choose a home nearby: "The great park of Berlin, the Tiergarten, close to the center of the city, is aristocratic in its look. Nursemaids wander in its fair but melancholy avenues, and lovers hold their trysts beneath its forest trees. Fine carriages roll along the level drive to Charlottenburg and horsemen canter in romantic groups along its green and winding alleys."[199]

She made her Viennese debut playing the Liszt E-flat Concerto with the Vienna Philharmonic Orchestra, Hans Richter conducting, in 1892 and the *Vienna Evening Post* remarked, "It is 'her' Liszt she played, and her own deep understanding of him has wedded her to his compositions."[200] One of the most distinguished Viennese musical critics, Edward Hanslick, called her "The queen of the Lisztian Amazons."[201] She returned to Vienna in February of 1896 where on the 13th she performed the Schumann Piano Quartet with the Bohemian String Quartet and a recital the following Monday, February 17.

In the summer of 1897 she played in London and wrote of it to Mrs. Gilder. "I hope you have passed your summer very agreeably. We were at first in England where I played in London (Philharmonic concert) and where it was positively delightful..."[202] This London Philharmonic concert featured a rare feat,

Neue Freie Presse, Vienna, February 16, 1896

even for today: two piano concertos in one evening. Even more remarkable is that both concertos were played back to back on the first half of the program. This concert, which must have been a great musical event for the British, was reported in the *London Times* on June 19, 1897.

As a special contribution to the commemoration to the 60 year's reign [of Queen Victoria, of course] the con-

cert given on Thursday night was of the length to which audiences were more accustomed at the beginning of the "Victorian" era than they are now . . . the performance of one symphony, two overtures, an orchestral fantasy, two concertos, and an extended vocal scena, without counting the performance of the National Anthem and the 15 minute interval . . . the work in concerto form was the masterpiece of Schumann, the piano part of which was played with consummate beauty of style by Fräulein aus der Ohe . . . She then chose a concerto by Liszt [the E-flat] . . . the young artist made an emphatic success . . .[203]

Upon her arrival in Rome, where she played her debut in April of 1898, she wrote this charming letter:

Roma, Italia
Pension Boos
Palazzo Rospigliosi
(Via del Quirinale e via Nazionale)
February 3rd, 1898

My dear Mrs. Gilder—
It is so long since I heard from you that I almost fear you have forgotten me! What as I hope, is not the case! . . . At present my sister and I are here. We have not seen much of the city yet, but expect wonders! And I am so delighted with the blue sky and the bright sun, which remind me so much of beautiful winter days in America. It seems such a relief as since some months we had persistently leaden sky in Germany, which

was almost unbearable. The sun only came out on half a dozen days since the end of October. I am going to play here too, if God wills it, and we hope to stay here until probably the middle of March . . . Now I must stop writing as I am still dreadfully fatigued from voyage and arrival, from which my handwriting gives ample proof. What a strange thing it is to be here in this old city! A world of thoughts crowd in upon one. I only hope and wish that people here might prove as musical and music loving as the place is interesting! I could not entirely appreciate all its beauties, were there no music in the air! From Mathilde and myself best regards to you and to Mr. Gilder . . .

Yours with love, Adele aus der Ohe

A second letter from Italy: "We have spent here a delightful time and enjoyed Rome immensely. Saturday last I played with the Societa Orchestrale Romana in one of their Symphony concerts. The Queen of Italy was present and spoke very graciously to me. She loves music very much."[204]

It was during this time in Italy that aus der Ohe learned of the sudden death of the great conductor Anton Seidl. Mr. Seidl first invited aus der Ohe to America for her debut concert and he had conducted many of her subsequent New York concerts. His death was a total shock and was attributed to ptomain poison from fish he ate at lunch. He had dined with his wife at 1:30 P.M. and began to feel ill about 5:00 P.M. By 7:00 P.M. a doctor was called, and by 10:15 P.M. "Mr. Seidl died in his wife's arms."[205]

"The death of Anton Seidl was the most serious blow that could have been struck at the musical life of this city at the present time...He has been the conductor of the Philharmonic Society, the Astoria subscription concerts, the Chickering Hall concerts, the entertainments of the Seidl Society, and of a series of Sunday night concerts at the Metropolitan Opera House..."[206] Aus der Ohe immediately wrote Mrs. Seidl, "It is with the greatest regret that I read in the newspaper about the death of your husband, something that utterly shocks me! Please allow me, on behalf of myself and my sister, to express our heartfelt sympathy concerning this irreplaceable loss!"[207]

In September 1898 The *New York Times* reported her return to America for another busy season.

FRÄULEIN AUS DER OHE HERE—With the approach of the musical season every incoming steamer from Europe has among its passengers some one of renown in this particular profession. Fräulein Adele aus der Ohe, the pianiste, returned to this country under the management of Henry Wolfsohn yesterday. She will make her first appearance at the Worcester Festival next Thursday afternoon, after which she will make a five weeks tour visiting Toronto, Oberlin, Ohio, where she will play for the Oberlin School of Music, and going from there to the Pacific Coast. She will return in time for her New York appearance with the New York Philharmonic Society at Carnegie Hall on November 4 and 5, after which she will be heard with the Boston Symphony Orchestra in this city, Boston, Providence, and Philadelphia.

She will also play with the Pittsburgh Orchestra under Victor Herbert's direction and then with the Thomas Orchestra in Chicago.[208]

The reviews were sensational. "In the piano field this season the women have evidently 'taken the palm.' Mme. Carreños' tour has been a regular ovation almost equaling Paderewski's reception during his appearance some time since. Another artist whose magnificent playing has compelled the most enthusiastic compliments from the critics is Miss aus der Ohe...She is one of the world's few absolutely great artists, those who never disappoint expectation, and who accomplish with splendid results every task which they undertake..."[209]

In November 1898, aus der Ohe appeared three times in New York City within that single month. She began on November 4 with a performance in Carnegie Hall of the Brahms Concerto No. 2 in B-flat with the Philharmonic Society, Emil Pauer conducting—her premiere performance of this great work. She followed with her customary two-recital series on November 15 and November 22, both at Mendelssohn Hall.

In a November 1895 letter, aus der Ohe had written a tantalizing comment: "Mathilde and I have returned yesterday from a trip to Dresden and Vienna, meeting in the latter city Brahms, with whom we had a long and interesting conversation. We told him much about America, what [sic] interested him greatly."[210]

What an experience that must have been—a visit with Brahms. He was, without a doubt, the greatest musician

Tuesday Afternoon, November 15,

AT 2.30.

PROGRAMME.

TOCCATA AND FUGUE — D minor, - - - - BACH-TAUSIG

SONATE — F minor, Op. 57, - - - - - - BEETHOVEN

> Allegro assai.
> Andante con moto.
> Allegro ma non troppo. Presto.

VARIATIONS SÉRIEUSES, - - - - - MENDELSSOHN

THREE ETUDES — Op. 25, Nos. 1, 2 and 3,

VALSE — A flat, Op. 42,   - - CHOPIN

ANDANTE AND POLONAISE,

BARCAROLLE, - - - - - - - RUBINSTEIN

MELODIE — Op. 4, No. 1,

                - - - - A. AUS DER OHE

ETUDE,

RHAPSODIE HONGROISE, No. 12, - - - - - LISZT

Tuesday Afternoon, November 22,

AT 2.30.

PROGRAMME.

SONATE—G minor, Op. 22,   -   -   -   -   -   -   Schumann

         Il più presto possibile.

         Andantino.

         Molto Allegro e marcato.

         Rondo.

PRELUDE APPASSIONATA,   -   -   -   -   -   H. H. Huss

"DIE HEILIGEN DREI BRUNNEN BEI TRAFOI,"

     ("The Sacred Three Springs near Trafoi,")   -   Franz Kullak

SUITE — E major, Op. 8, (First time,)   -   -   -   A. Aus der Ohe

        Prélude.   Sarabande.   À la Bourrée.

        Air.   Gavotte.   Gigue.

TWO SONGS WITHOUT WORDS,

        No. 1. F major.   No. 2. Spinning Song.   }   Mendelssohn

PRESTO — Op. 7,

NOCTURNE — F minor, Op. 55, No. 1,   -   -   -   -   Chopin

VALSE–CAPRICE,   -   -   -   -   -   -   -   -   Tausig

NOCTURNE,   }

TARANTELLE DI BRAVURA, }   -   -   -   -   Liszt

alive. At the time of this meeting, Brahms was sixty-two years old and nearing the end of his life—he died less than two years later, in April of 1897. He had already written all that he was to write for the piano. Even the great miniatures of his final years (Ops. 116, 117, 118, 119) were complete.

When aus der Ohe first performed Brahms' great Second Piano Concerto in B-flat in 1898, it was one year after Brahms' death and only seventeen years after Brahms had completed it, in 1881. Did she possibly discuss the concerto with Brahms during her 1895 visit with him? Did Brahms possibly express a desire to have her play it? Or perhaps the inspiration to perform it came after his death as a tribute to this profoundly important musician and composer.

This concerto is one of Brahms' largest and most important compositions as well as one of the longest and most difficult piano concertos ever written. When reading about aus der Ohe's performances of it, I am reminded of the Chinese proverb: "The person who says it cannot be done should not interrupt the person doing it!" People were constantly amazed that a woman could play such a long and demanding piece of music, and some went so far as to state that it was simply an impossibility for a woman; but play it she did, and by all accounts she played it beautifully—it must have suited her perfectly.

Miss aus der Ohe played the beautiful concerto with its wealth of melody and romantic feeling like the sterling artist that she is. Not a measure stinted, not a scale

*treated as if it were but remplissage. Everything was
noble and elevated in feeling.* [211]

It was also in 1898 that the Gilders purchased Four
Brooks Farm in Tyringham, Massachusetts, located in
the Berkshire Mountains about 125 miles west of Boston.
They began to spend their summers at this farm and enter-
tained many guests, including President and Mrs. Grover
Cleveland. With aus der Ohe's deep love of nature, this
rural retreat must have proved a restful haven for her and
Mathilde. In response to an invitation to visit, aus der Ohe
replied to Mrs. Gilder.

> *. . . But we were so delighted to hear from you again and
> I hasten to write to you now, thanking you most kindly
> for your letter and your kind invitation to come and see
> you at your farm. We should love to do so and I believe
> we could arrange very well to come . . . and stay for a
> few days. We could never find it dull where you are . . .* [212]

Following one of these delightful visits aus der Ohe
wrote,

> *. . . we are back in the fascinating centre of American
> life. But my mind returns often to the loveliness of
> Tyringham, which forever is imprinted into my mem-
> ory. And could I ever think of it without remembering
> all your kindness and love, shown to myself and my
> sisters? Let me again thank you with all my heart in my
> name and in the name of my dear ones . . .*

We found a great deal to attend to in New York, so that it was really necessary to be here, although hard to leave Tyringham while you were still there.

Kindest regards to all of you from my sisters and me.

Auf glückliches Wiedersehen in New York, wenn Gott will. In herzlicher Liebe and Dankbarkeit.[In hopes of a glad reunion in New York, if God wills. With heartfelt love and gratitude.] [213]

Adele aus der Ohe at Four Brooks Farm
Courtesy The Lilly Library, Indiana University, Bloomington, Indiana

In Boston in 1899, she delivered a veritable aus der Ohe festival—four appearances within the span of one week. She began on February 11 (as she had the previous year in New York) with the Brahms Concerto No. 2 in B-flat with the Boston Symphony, Wilhelm Gericke conducting.

> Brahm's B-flat Concerto strikes one more and more as a great work of true genius . . . The pianoforte part in this concerto is enormously, almost inordinately difficult technically, but it is not in the least showy; the pianist who demands something more than fine music to play will inevitably find it rather thankless. To the pianist, on the other hand, who asks for nothing more than intrinsically great and beautiful music to play, this work is as noble a task as can be found in the modern literature of the instrument. Miss aus der Ohe played it admirably indeed . . . hers was profound, thoughtful, soulful playing; well rounded in conception, strong and clear in execution; it was all on a grand, heroic scale, with an exquisite touch of poetry at the right moments. Miss aus der Ohe impresses one more and more as a true artist of very high rank; she is eminently one of the great ones.[214]

This was followed by an appearance at a chamber music concert given by the Kneisel Quartet on February 13. Aus der Ohe performed the Franck Sonata for violin and piano with Franz Kneisel as the violinist. She then presented the following program at her first solo recital on February 15 at Steinert Hall:

SCHUMANN	SONATA IN G MINOR OP. 22
MENDELSSOHN	TWO SONGS WITHOUT WORDS
POLDINI	*IDYLLE* OP. 23 NO. 1
WILLIAM MASON	ALBUM LEAF IN E-FLAT
AUS DER OHE	SUITE NO. 2 IN E MAJOR OP. 8
CHOPIN	NOCTURNE IN C# MINOR OP. 27 NO. 1
	VALSE IN E MINOR
LISZT	*ETUDE DE CONCERT* IN D-FLAT
	POLONAISE IN E MAJOR

She followed up with this second program on February 18, also at Steinert Hall.

BEETHOVEN	SONATA IN E-FLAT OP. 31 NO. 3
BACH/SAINT SAENS	GAVOTTE IN B MINOR
BACH	FRENCH SUITE IN G MAJOR NO. 5
CHOPIN	NOCTURNE IN F MINOR OP. 55 NO. 1
TCHAIKOVSKY	THEME AND VARIATIONS OP. 19
AUS DER OHE	MELODY OP. 4
	ETUDE OP. 3
LISZT	NOCTURNE NO. 1
	TARANTELLA DI BRAVURA

Within the span of one week she had performed one of the most difficult piano concertos ever written, followed by a chamber concert appearance in one of the major works of that repertoire, and then followed with her customary two solo recitals—already an amazing accomplishment—but that was not all. Ten days later she gave a third solo recital, on February 28, at Association Hall.

BEETHOVEN	SONATA IN F MINOR OP. 57
	APPASSIONATA
AUS DER OHE	SUITE NO. 2 IN E MAJOR OP. 8
MENDELSSOHN	SONGS WITHOUT WORDS
CHOPIN	ETUDES OP. 25 NO. 1, 2, 3
TAUSIG	*VALSE CAPRICE*
RUBINSTEIN	*BARCAROLLE* IN F MINOR
LISZT	HUNGARIAN RHAPSODY NO. 12

What a series this must have been for Boston music lovers—a wonderfully munificent musical gift to a city she adored and that adored her in return. It would have been something to hear.

Whenever aus der Ohe presented multiple recitals such as these, she was careful never to repeat works. Notice, however, in these Boston programs that she played her Suite No. 2 at both her February 15 and February 28 recitals. According to the review of the February 28 recital, "Her suite, played by request, gained on second hearing."[215]

The concert season of 1899–1900 was an unfortunate one for aus der Ohe. She was forced to cancel all of her American engagements. Her sister Mathilde wrote,

We were so sorry to not be in America this season, but my
sister was ill in November just at about the time we had
to leave with the steamer, to be there in time for her con-
certs. My sister was engaged to play in Boston with the
Boston Symphony... and also to play with the Orches-
tra on the tour... You can imagine how sorry she was
that she had to give up all these concerts and of course
many other concerts besides, on account of illness; she
had the grip. We hope to be in America next year...[216]

Aus der Ohe played concerts in Germany that season,
including "a recital in Berlin, the program consisting entirely
of her own compositions,"[217] and a concert in Potsdam where
she played before Her Majesty, the Empress of Germany. In a
letter dated September 26, 1900, Mathilde reported,

We also spent this summer a delightful time in Wei-
mar where my sister played and where she had the
great distinction and honor, that His Royal Highness
the Grand Duke of Saxe-Weimar gave her the title of
"großherzogliche-sächsische Hofpianistin," that is
Court Pianist to His Royal Highness the Grand Duke of
Saxe-Weimar. The title was conferred upon her, as the
diploma says, in recognition of her excellent achieve-
ments in musical art.[218]

It must have been very gratifying for aus der Ohe to
receive this honor in a city that was the source of such
important and pleasant memories. Weimar had been the

summer home of Franz Liszt for the last twenty-five years of his life, and aus der Ohe had studied with Liszt in Weimar for nearly half of those years. Undoubtedly, every street and alley of this small, charming city was familiar to her and brought back memories of those glorious student days.

She was named Court Pianist to the Duke of Saxony-Anhalt in 1905 and was further honored in 1907 when Kaiser Wilhelm II gave her the title Royal Prussian Court Pianist, a title once held by her great teacher Theodor Kullak.

Adele and Mathilde returned once more to America for the 1900–1901 season but this journey proved to be ill-fated.

The four Ohe siblings were an unusually closely bonded family, no doubt at least partially due to having lost their parents so early in their lives. Aus der Ohe somewhat jokingly confessed in a letter to Mrs. Gilder: "you know how we three sisters cling to each other."[219] When the inevitable illnesses and eventual deaths of these siblings began to occur, aus der Ohe felt the losses keenly. The first crack in this extremely solid family bond occurred in March of 1901, while Adele and Mathilde were in the midst of their American tour. The *New York Times* reported, "Miss Adele aus der Ohe, the pianist, was called to her home in Berlin this week by the sickness of her sister, and therefore cancelled her tour, which was to have kept her in this country until the early part of May. She sailed on the Majestic."[220]

A sense of the palpable anxiety they experienced while sailing back to Europe comes from a letter to Mrs. Gilder. "... my sister Fernande was better when we reached home, as also a letter had informed us already when we reached Liverpool. You cannot imagine what a relief this welcome letter was for us, when we reached England, after having endured the suspense of this trip in the uncertainty of the thought: will we find Fernande alive, or gone already?"[221]

Adele and Mathilde remained in Europe for the rest of 1901. They returned to London in November, from where she wrote, "Mathilde and I are in London as you see. I am to play some recitals in December ... we are to be here till about the middle of next month, when we go to Brussels ... My recitals are to be December 5th and 9th at Steinway Hall. I shall play at my recitals also some of my own works."[222]

Her London program of December 5 consisted of:

SCHUMANN	SONATA IN G MINOR
AUS DER OHE	SUITE IN E MAJOR
	SPINNING SONG
	LEGENDE
	VALSE
	ETUDE
CHOPIN	SONATA IN B-FLAT MINOR
SCHUBERT	IMPROMPTU
LISZT	NOCTURNE
	HUNGARIAN RHAPSODY No. 12

This program is unique in that about one quarter of it is given over to her own works. Aside from the Berlin recital noted earlier that consisted entirely of her compositions, this is possibly the largest amount of her own music that aus der Ohe ever programmed in a single concert. It is a testament to her growing confidence as a composer as well as to the ever-increasing receptiveness of her audiences to her music. The British press was pleased. The *Morning Post* reported, "At her recital yesterday she not only appeared as an executant, but introduced several compositions of her own, revealing great talent..."[223] And *The Era:* "...proved herself a pianist of a superior kind...Her gifts are remarkable...We take leave of the lady with hearty wishes for her future success, her abilities being so striking. English audiences may appear cold to strangers, but their attitude changes altogether when talent like that of this lady appeals to them."[224]

From London, Adele and Mathilde traveled to Belgium where she wrote on December 14, "Last night I played here in Brussels...and two days before at a court concert...I received today a beautiful brooch of diamonds and pearls from Her Royal Highness the Princess of Flanders. Isn't it a beautiful souvenir?"[225]

She was planning a return to America for the 1902 season, writing in her characteristic manner, "I think I shall be there after Christmas, if God will..."

Unfortunately this time God did not will—for her brother Gustav died suddenly. Very little is known about him except that he was a noted painter and had, in 1890, received the first prize at the Royal Academy of Arts in Berlin for his painting "Pieta."[226] Showings of his art had occurred in both Germany and America.

We know nothing of his untimely death except that he was only fifty years old. It was a terrible blow to the three sisters and triggered a great upheaval in their lives. Aus der

Ohe played no concerts from the time of her brother's death in 1902 until the fall of 1903. Her grief was profound and even as late as 1904, two years after his death, several of aus der Ohe's letters are edged in black as a sign of mourning. In a thank-you note to Mrs. Gilder, she writes, "We have received some time ago the charming silver things you gave us on my birthday, all signed with our names. Thank you so much. They have given us so much pleasure and will always be a pleasant remembrance of a day that was pleasant through your love and kindness, although overshadowed by old and new grief."[227]

In her grief, aus der Ohe turned to her art for consolation. Her final published work, published in 1906, the Violin and Piano Sonata in F-sharp, bears the inscription "*Dem Andenken meines Bruders Gustav aus der Ohe*" (In memory of my brother Gustav aus der Ohe). This dedication of a work

for piano and violin might very well be an indication that Gustav was a violinist as well as a painter. Perhaps, while writing this Sonata, she was remembering earlier days when she accompanied her brother.

At some point after the death of their brother, the three sisters made a decision to move to America. Adele and Mathilde vacated their lovely home on Ansbacherstrasse and

Braut auf dem Hofplatz (Bride in the Courtyard). Oil on canvas, 1897, painted by Gustav aus der Ohe

Fernande vacated the home in Zehlendorf bei Berlin, the family home that she and Gustav had shared since the death of their parents almost twenty years earlier.

In the fall of 1903, Adele and Mathilde, now accompanied by their sister Fernande, sailed for America after an absence of nearly two-and-a-half years. Their move to America was widely reported at the time. "The fact that Miss aus der Ohe has become a resident of America should be a cause for rejoicing for everyone who is interested in the musical development of this country, as she is indeed, a rare artist..."[228]

At the time of her return to America in 1903, aus der Ohe was forty-two years old. She had been touring and performing for nearly her entire life, as far east as Moscow and St. Petersburg and as far west as Los Angeles and San Francisco. Her music-making represented the culmination of a lifetime of incredible work and study as well as nearly a lifetime of public performance. She must have felt a real sense of satisfaction as she read, in the *Chicago Daily Tribune*, this lovely article:

> ...*the patrons of the Hamlin concert at the Grand yesterday afternoon were permitted to enjoy some noble piano playing. Adele aus der Ohe had not been heard here before in nearly a decade, and doubtless to many of her auditors she came as a complete stranger. Those who remembered her recalled with pleasure playing that was technically complete, and interpretively admirable for the musical thoroughness and artistic sincerity that distinguishes it. But the years have been*

known to bring about marked changes in makers of melody, and it therefore was not without some curiosity that former admirers of Miss aus der Ohe's playing awaited her appearance before them.

She came.

They saw a slender, black robed figure, the blond hair a few shades darker than was last seen, and worn now, not in a braid, as it was then, but done in soft curls about the head. Otherwise there was but little change in appearance; slightly mature, it is true, but the same quiet, gracious, refined manner that has ever spoken of a nature and origin truly aristocratic, and the same directness of going to the task at hand that has always been noted.

And the playing?

The years have brought to full and fine fruition the splendid promise their predecessors contained. Miss aus der Ohe today is just as thoroughly satisfying a pianist and artist as the lover of good, honest, genuine music could ask to hear. She is exceptionally equipped in all essentials. Her touch never for an instant loses its velvety roundness and beauty, no matter whether it be heard in the finest pianissimo or in the most brilliant bravura. It is a tone which has body, solidity, surety, and an invariably noble quality. It is heard in everything done—in a scale which is delightfully even, limpid, and fleet. In the smooth legato in which a melody is voiced, in trills, in arpeggios or embellishments admirably clear and exact, in chords splendidly solid and firm, and even in strong ringing octaves which that remarkable left hand sends sweeping up from the bass or which come crashing down from the treble. Everything is tonally beautiful, and therein lies one of the unfailing charms of Miss aus der Ohe's performance. Technically she is equal to all demands modern piano playing makes on its devotees.

The Beethoven Variations were as admirable technically as they were musically. The clarity in phrasing, the exactness in pedaling, the fine sense of tonal and dynamic proportion—these were as eminently satisfying as were the honesty and sincerity of musical purpose displayed in the reading accorded the interesting work. The Liszt Tarantella showed the player in the true virtuoso light, and here again all was technically exceptional. There was no show for show's sake, for there was a poise, a surety, and an authority in every phrase which made it seem that difficult did not exist, and that nothing unusual was being accomplished. But those who knew realized they were listening to a performance superb in its bravour and extraordinary in its breadth and its brilliancy. One of Schubert's longest and rarest heard impromptus was played with so much of contrast and variety, such clever employment of sharp accents and rhythm that it took on interest and charm. An original "Legend" of much poetic suggestiveness was beautifully delivered. One of the least known of the Chopin waltzes had inspiring buoyancy and crispness to make it attractive, and Liszt's "Waldesrauschen" given with exquisite tonal beauty, a stirring Etude evidently

*of original composition, and the first number from
Liszt's "Consolation" were among the encores played by
this excellent pianist, musician, and artist.*[229]

A Boston article of 1904 closed with this summation:

*If Miss aus der Ohe had sought relief for her emotions
in another art, she would have been a sculptor, not a
painter. The line and the chasteness of marble appeal
to her more than the perishable tints and the proud
sumptuousness of the flesh. In the great Valhalla there
are rooms for all that truly follow art. Some of these
rooms are filled with men and women whose artistic
expression is common to them all. Miss aus der Ohe has
a room to herself, for we know of no pianist, male or
female, who has her characteristics.*[230]

Aus der Ohe was in great demand upon her return
to America. She traveled extensively and played many
concerts between the years 1903 to 1906. *The Music Trade
Review* observed, "Adele aus der Ohe has a few weeks of tremendous work before her and she has been playing with the
greatest orchestras of the country ever since the season's
opening."[231] The magazine further noted, "It is unnecessary
to tell of the success and art of Carreño, Bloomfield-Zeisler,
Rive-King, aus der Ohe. These names are household words
in America, and each holds her own this season."[232] "Adele
aus der Ohe is making a furor this season by her wonderfully beautiful pianism . . ."[233] Adele herself wrote Mrs. Gil-

der in April of 1904, "I would have sent you our thanks long before but was tremendously busy."[234]

The milestone of passing from one century into another is always a time for reflection, both on what has passed and on what may be. This was true in modern times as we recently passed into the twenty-first century and it was certainly true in the early years of the 1900s as Americans entered the twentieth century. *The Music Trade Review* published just such a commentary in 1904.

> *The development of an art is of slow growth and not often is it within the power of anyone to point directly to the influences which have made for the betterment of conditions until years have closed behind . . . It seems fit that an era or an epoch should make itself felt in the opening years of the twentieth century and if we can only realize that this is upon us at the present moment, perhaps we can further its influence and its force.*
>
> *The influence of the pianist is perhaps deeper and more subtle than that of any other individual, because in the piano lies the concentrated essence of all music. It is the instrument which stands for every voice in the orchestra. The man who plays it represents conductor and each individual instrument, and upon him rests the responsibility of unfolding its beauties, as also the meanings of the works which he interprets.*
>
> *. . . The pianists who have helped to make the [1904] season have been of remarkable proportions, and in the combination [of these various pianists] those who could understand must have seen that as*

contrasts and as examples of the different elements in the art of piano playing we may never again have such valuable studies. Bauer, Busoni, and Reisenauer— Adele aus der Ohe and Fannie Bloomfield-Zeisler. In addition to this galaxy—Joseffy!

Each of these artists is a painter in tone, and from no two have we heard the same tonal effects. This means clearly that the piano is "All things unto all men . . ."[235]

The prescience of this article is remarkable, for indeed the opening of the twentieth century was a "Golden Age" for piano. Quite possibly there will never again be such examples of the different elements of piano artistry—d'Albert, Bauer, Bloomfield-Zeisler, Busoni, Carreño, Friedheim, Gabrilowitsch, Godowsky, Hofmann, Joseffy, Lhevinne, aus der Ohe, Pachmann, Paderewski, Rachmaninoff, Reisenauer, Rive-King, Rosenthal, Sauer, Siloti—all (and many more) were performing in the early years of the twentieth century. It was a pianistic wealth of embarrassing proportions.

An important year for aus der Ohe, 1906 marked the twentieth anniversary of her phenomenal American debut of December 1886. She began this celebratory year with January performances in her two favorite American cities—New York and Boston. In New York she played the Tchaikovsky Concerto with the Philharmonic Society, Vasily Safonoff conducting. The *New York Times* noted, ". . . she has seldom played it with such a sweep of sonorous power, such elasticity and brilliance, such poetry; and she seemed infected with the glowing enthusiasm of the conductor. She, too, was richly rewarded with applause and admiration."[236]

In Boston, she played the Beethoven Concerto No. 5 in E-flat. "Beethoven's noble work was finely interpreted by Miss aus der Ohe ... the audience cordially greeted the artist and insistently recalled her at the close of her performance..."[237] Her longtime friend, Wilhelm Gericke, who had returned to his post as music director of the Boston Symphony in 1898 after several years in Europe, led the orchestra, an orchestra that she knew so well, loved so dearly, and had played with so many times. In fact, this was her fifty-first performance[238] with this venerable organization—a near record. Only a very, very small number of artists have appeared more times with the Boston Symphony, and no other pianist in the history of this orchestra comes even close to this number of performances. (It is a curious coincidence that, though neither of them knew it at the time, this was to be the final season with the Boston Symphony for both Miss aus der Ohe and Mr. Gericke. At the end of the season, Mr. Gericke resigned his post and returned to Europe, and at the end of the summer aus der Ohe also returned to Europe.)

Over the course of the past twenty years, aus der Ohe had traveled widely throughout the United States as well as Europe and Russia. She had played in many, many cities, often returning to the same cities multiple times for return engagements. She had performed as soloist with all the major American orchestras as well as most of the major orchestras of Europe and Russia, including the Royal Orchestra in Berlin, the Vienna Philharmonic, the London Philharmonic, the Moscow Philharmonic, the Imperial Russian Music Society in St. Petersburg, the Societa Orchestrale in Rome, and the Gewandhaus in Leipzig.

She played before her Majesty the Empress Frederick of Germany, the Empress Augusta Victoria, the King and Queen of Saxony, the Grand Duke of Saxe-Weimar, Queen Margherita of Italy, the Crown Princess Stephanie of Austria, the Duke and Duchess of Cumberland, and the Duchess of Holstein, the mother of the German Empress.

Her popularity had never waned, and year after year she remained in high demand. As she contemplated her twenty-year anniversary, she might easily have looked back with great satisfaction to the many important musical events she had been privileged to be a part of.

Aus der Ohe had become an integral part of musical history both in America and Europe. She had been frequently called upon when the occasion required an especially significant performance. She participated in the opening of Carnegie Hall, played in the opening season of both the Chicago Symphony and the Minneapolis Symphony, and played the inaugural concert for the Schubert Club of St. Paul, Minnesota. In London she had participated in the Jubilee concert honoring sixty years of Queen Victoria's reign, and in Berlin she had participated in the 400th Jubilee concert of the Royal Orchestra.

She had worked with all the great conductors of her time, including Tchaikovsky, Vassily Safonoff, Hans Richter, Emil Paur, and Arthur Nikisch; but it was the conductors in America—Wilhelm Gericke in Boston, Theodore Thomas in Chicago, and Walter Damrosch in New York—with whom she formed the deepest bonds of admiration and affection.

She had much to be grateful for and, at the mere age of forty-five, had much more to look forward to when, suddenly and tragically, disaster struck on August 20, 1906.

Miss Mathilde aus der Ohe, sister of Adele aus der Ohe, the celebrated pianist, died at the Raleigh Hotel this morning from heart disease. Her two sisters were with her. They were born in the Province of Hanover, Germany, and their home is in Berlin.

Miss Mathilde aus der Ohe had long been a chaperon for her sister, the pianist, and had accompanied her in all her concert tours. For several summers they had been at Lake Mohegan and Peekskill. [239]

The Misses Mathilde and Adele aus der Ohe went to New York on June 29 for a few hours, and, while returning, Miss Mathilde was stricken with paralysis. She recovered from this ailment and also from an attack of pneumonia, but the illness affected her heart and indirectly led to her death. [240]

And then, inevitably,

Miss Adele aus der Ohe, the pianist sailed for Europe yesterday [August 28] on the steamship Bremen, taking the body of her sister, Miss Mathilde, who died in their summer home at Peekskill (New York) on August 20. The funeral will be held in Berlin. Miss aus der Ohe had arranged a tour of this country beginning early in the fall but her manager, Henry Wolfsohn, said she would

not be seen on the concert stage for some time, and that
many of her dates must be cancelled.[241]

Her sister had been her constant traveling companion
and the loss was devastating. Mathilde was only fifty-five
years old at the time of her death and she and Adele had
been inseparable their entire lives. They were traveling
together as early as 1874 and after thirty years it was impossible for aus der Ohe to function without her sister, both
physically and emotionally. The physical work of traveling
in those days with the sort of grueling schedule aus der Ohe
was accustomed to required two people, and also the life of
a performing musician is one of emotional intensity. One
needs a strong support system to navigate the complexities
of stage life. Mathilde had been a surrogate mother, business partner, career consultant, travel agent, secretary,
counselor, friend and confidant, and probably much more.
She was, simply, irreplaceable.

Ilsenburg am Harz
November 2nd, [19]06

Dear Mrs. Gilder
I have written Mr. Gilder some days ago to thank him
for his sympathy in the loss of my sister and the letter
which I only received in Germany, but I feel that I must
write to you too, thanking you for your kind messages
and for the hospitality Fernande and I have had at
your New York home the day before our sad departure
for Germany. You may be <u>sure</u> that we have appreciated
your kindness and your sympathy very much.

. . . What the loss of my sister has been to me I am sure you will guess. I am heartbroken, as you may imagine.

In my great sorrow it was a comfort and a consolation to find, also in Germany, so much sympathy and to see how warmly Mathilde's beautiful, lovely nature has been appreciated and loved. Among the expressions and messages of sympathy there was one also from Her Royal Highness the Countess of Trani, Duchess of Bavaria (sister of Elisabeth, Empress of Austria) that especially pleased me. Also my friend Frau von Hindenburg, geb. Gräfin zu Münster,[242] wrote me very beautifully about Mathilde, saying of her: ein Genie der Liebe and Hingabe; ich hatte wahre Ehrfurcht und Freundschaft fur sie. ["A genius of love and devotion; I had true respect and friendship for her"]. A few days ago Frau von Hindenburg wrote me again and sent me in her letter a passage from the works of Goethe, saying that in reading that passage she thought of myself and "meinen Schutzengel [my guardian angel] Mathilde." That passage of Goethe is very beautiful. I shall copy it out for you and send it enclosed; please do show it to Mr. Gilder and explain it to him in English . . . I hope you will let me hear once again from you, to tell me how you are. And keep always in loving remembrance her—Mathilde—whose memory is sacred to my heart.

With kindest regards to you and to Mr. Gilder from Fernande and me.

Affectionately yours,
Adele aus der Ohe

From the works of Goethe:

Das ist der Vorzug edler Naturen, daß ihr Hinscheiden in höhere Regionen segnend wirkt, wie ihr Verweilen auf der Erde; daß sie uns von dorther gleich Sternen entgegenleuchten, als Richtpunkte, wohin wir unsern Lauf bei einer nur zu oft durch Stürme unterbrochenen Fahrt zu richten haben, daß diejenigen, zu denen wir uns als zu Wohlwollenden und Hilfreichen im Leben hinwendeten, nun die sehnsuchtsvollen Blicke nach sich ziehen als Vollendete, Selige.

[This is the virtue of noble natures: that their departure to higher regions acts as a blessing, akin to their abidance on Earth, and that they shine to us thence like stars, as beacons that we can steer towards in our course, a journey all too often interrupted by storms, so that those to whom we turned in life as benevolent and helpful now draw longing gazes to themselves as ones who are consummate, blessed.][243]

Aus der Ohe had wonderful friends in America and she received many letters of sympathy and consolation. Two such friends were Edward and Marion MacDowell.

The great American pianist and composer Edward MacDowell had also, in his youth, studied piano with Liszt. MacDowell took his First Piano Concerto to one of his lessons. Eugene d'Albert happened to also be there at the time. Liszt asked MacDowell to play the concerto for him and asked d'Albert to play the orchestral part on a second piano.

When they finished Liszt was so pleased with the piece that he turned to d'Albert and said, "You must bestir yourself if you do not wish to be outdone by our young American."[244] D'Albert had an immediate dislike of MacDowell. Even years later, when d'Albert married his second wife (of six), the Venezuelan pianist Teresa Carreño (for her, d'Albert was third out of four husbands), d'Albert insisted she drop the MacDowell concerto from her repertoire.

MacDowell dedicated his First Piano Concerto to Liszt and Liszt graciously wrote: "I accept the dedication of your concerto with sincere pleasure and thanks."[245]

Upon his return to America, MacDowell settled in Boston and became one of the most respected composers in America.

By 1904 Edward MacDowell was suffering from a gradually increasing dementia, which had ended his career and was causing him to lose his mental capacities. That same year he was run over by a horse-drawn carriage and this accident seemed to accelerate his deterioration. Lawrence Gilman, his biographer, described him: "His mind became as that of a little child. He sat quietly, day after day, in a chair by a window, smiling patiently from time to time at those about him, turning the pages of a book of fairy tales that seemed to give him a definite pleasure, and greeting with a fugitive gleam of recognition certain of his more intimate friends."[246]

In the fall of 1907, aus der Ohe sent a hauntingly beautiful letter to Mrs. MacDowell. Aus der Ohe's letter, a response to a letter of condolence Mrs. MacDowell had sent in memory of Mathilde, reads as a reciprocal condolence letter but in fact Edward MacDowell was still alive, albeit in very poor condition, at the time of this letter. He died in January 1908, just a few months after aus der Ohe wrote to his wife Marion.

———————

Berlin W. 15,
Pariser Strasse 6,
Oct. 4th [19]07

My dear Mrs. MacDowell:
Forgive me that only at so late a date I reply to your letter. I thank you with all my heart for your sympathy, and I often thought whether in your own sorrow you might have heard of mine. I knew, before your letter came, that if you had heard of it, you would feel with me.

How vividly I recall the day when my beloved sister and I went to see you and saw, for the last time, also your dear husband. How it all came back to me when a little while ago I read in Mathilde's diary and found there mention of our visit to you, with tender and sympathetic words.

How I wish that God may give you strength to bear your heavy burden. How I wish that He may comfort and strengthen us both. Life, of course, can never be the same again to either of us; but out of all sorrow and despair there rises with almost overpowering intensity the hope, nay, the certainty (I venture to say) that we shall all meet again and that death itself cannot part those who truly love.—

Und Gott wird abwischen
alle Tränen von ihren
Augen."
[and God shall wipe all tears from their eyes]

These sacred words, which often have been a balm to
my own broken heart, I am sending you as a message
from my heart to yours. May they bring you the comfort
they often brought to me when I thought of my loved
ones and of the time when we shall all be together
again.

With warmest regards and loving sympathy to you,
dear friend, I am

Affectionately yours,
Adele aus der Ohe

The death of Mathilde was a loss from which she could
not recover, for Adele aus der Ohe never returned to
America.

Berlin W. 15,
Pariser Strasse 6,
Oct. 4ᵗʰ 07.

My dear Mrs. MacDowell:

Forgive me that only
at so late a date I reply
to your letter. I thank
you with all my heart for
your sympathy; and
I often thought, whether
in your own sorrow
you might have heard
of mine. I knew, before
your letter came, that
if you had heard of it,
you would feel with me.

How vividly — I recall the
day when my beloved sister
and I went to see you
and saw, for the last time,
also your dear husband.
How it all came back to me
when a little while ago I read
in Mathildes diary and found
there mention of our visit
to you, with tender and
sympathetic words.
How I wish that God may
give you strength to bear
your heavy burden. How
I wish that He may comfort
and strengthen us both.
Life, of course, can never be

the same again to either
of us; but out of all sorrow
and despair there rises
with almost overpowering intensity
the hope, nay, the certainty
(I venture to say,) that we shall
all meet again and that death
itself cannot part those who
truly love. –

„Und Gott wird abwischen
„alle Tränen von ihren
„Augen."

These sacred words, which often
have been a balm to my own
broken heart, I am sending you
as a message from my heart
to yours. May they bring you
the comfort they often brought
to me when I thought

of my loved ones and of the time when we shall all be together again. —

With warmest regards and loving sympathy to you, dear friend, I am

Affectionately yours
Adele aus der Ohe.

Courtesy of Boston Public Library

Berlin

In January 1909, New Year greetings from Berlin arrived in New York.

My dear Mrs. Gilder

This is to bring you my warmest congratulations for your coming birthday, but also for the New Year that just commenced. May it be a very happy one for you and all those whom you love.

Tell Mr. Gilder that I am delighted with his "Complete Works." It is more than a pleasure to have all his poems in one volume, all those I know so well, and the new ones: "In Helena's Garden" added to them.

It is long since I heard from you and I hope you will now let me hear from you before long. I have myself been very very busy with my art. Work is a great consolation; these last years would have taught me this, had I not known it before.

With kindest love believe me always
Yours affectionately,
Adele aus der Ohe[247]

This was the last time aus der Ohe was able to send greetings to Richard Gilder, for he died later that year. It is impossible that letters of condolence and consolation did not pass between these two friends, but whatever letters Mrs. Gilder received from aus der Ohe have not been preserved for public consumption—I am quite sure they were too personal and painful to be shared.

The year 1910 brought yet more tragedy.

On August 12, at 3:45 in the morning, God took to
himself my dearly beloved, precious sister, Luise
Fernande aus der Ohe of Barenfels near Kipsdorf in the
Saxon Ore Mountains into His heavenly kingdom after
prolonged, difficult suffering. This announcement is
being made by sole surviving, most deeply grieving

Adele aus der Ohe
Royal Prussian Court Pianist
Berlin W. 15, end of August 1910
Pariser Strasse 6
Thank you for refraining from wreath donations and
sympathy visits.

The funeral and burial quietly took place on
August 20 in Berlin at the Old Jerusalem Cemetery,

Au 3

Am 12. August morgens 3 ³/₄ Uhr nahm Gott meine heissgeliebte, teure Schwester

Luise Fernande aus der Ohe

zu Bärenfels bei Kipsdorf im sächs. Erzgebirge nach längeren schweren Leiden sanft zu Sich in Sein himmlisches Reich.

Dies zeigt, allein zurückgeblieben, in tiefstem Schmerze an

Adele aus der Ohe
Königl. Preuss. Hofpianistin.

BERLIN W. 15, Ende August 1910
Pariser Strasse 6.

Kranzspenden und Beileidsbesuche dankend verbeten.

Die Trauerfeier und Beerdigung fand am 20. August zu Berlin auf dem Alten Jerusalemer Kirchhof, Belle-Alliance-Strasse, dem Wunsche der teuren Verewigten entsprechend in aller Stille statt.

Belle-Alliance Street, in accordance with the wish of
the deceased loved one.

Luise Fernande was sixty-one years old. Gustav had been only fifty and Mathilde fifty-five at the time of their deaths. The Ohe children had been given many blessings but longevity was not one of them. Only Adele would enjoy a lifespan exceeding that of her parents.

At the time of Luise Fernande's death, Adele was living at 6 Pariser Strasse, her third and final Berlin residence. The American journalist Harriett Brower visited aus der Ohe and later wrote, "Another opportunity to see the home of an artist was afforded me when Frl. aus der Ohe invited me to visit her in her Berlin home. She also lives in the newer western portion of the city, where so many other artists are located. One feels on entering the spacious rooms that this home has the true German atmosphere. Several paintings of large size and striking originality hang on the walls of the pianist's home. They all illustrate religious themes and are the work of Herr aus der Ohe, the pianist's only brother, who passed away at the height of his career."[248]

As always, aus der Ohe remained stoically busy. The Woman's Lyceum was an important project. The Women's Lyceum Clubs were founded in 1902 in London as an antidote to the male-only clubs that were then prevalent. Women were beginning to move into the male-dominated professional world and these clubs were founded on the belief that women were entitled to "a professional life and full freedom of development."[249] The Berlin chapter was established in November 1905. The intent was to "build centers of intellectual and artistic life in order to promote exchange between cultivated women of all nations."[250]

Miss aus der Ohe had much to relate of the Woman's Lyceum. The Department of Music was founded by aus der Ohe herself. Not long ago there was an exhibition of woman's work in music. Women composers from all over the country sent examples of their work. Our own Mrs. H.A.A. Beach, who has been located for some time in Munich, was well represented. There are branches of this institution in other German cities.[251]

Amy Beach (1867–1944) was a New England musician and longtime acquaintance of aus der Ohe. Mrs. Beach was one of the first successful American female composers and aus der Ohe strongly supported her work.

Dear Mrs. Beach
The Deutsch Lyceum Club of Berlin gives a large exhibition in this city from February to March 1912, about which the enclosed printed material will give you information. The music department will exhibit also compositions by Women Composers and should be very much pleased if also you would exhibit some of your works. If you will do so—and we hope you will—kindly fill out the enclosed "Fragebogen" [questionnaire] and send it at your <u>earliest</u> convenience. Could you let us have also a picture of yours for the exhibition? We should be very much pleased if you could.

It gave me so much pleasure to have your Violin-Sonata performed at one of our concerts, the season before last.

With kindest regards
Very sincerely yours,
Adele aus der Ohe
Vorsitzende der Musikabteilung der Ausstellung des Deutscher Lyceum Club in Berlin
(Chairman of the Music Division of the Exhibitions of the German Lyceum Club in Berlin)[252]

In October 1911 aus der Ohe received news of Mrs. Gilder's European trip and dashed off this plea for a visit. It is the last surviving letter between these two longtime and cherished friends.

My dearest Mrs. Gilder,
Mr. Bagby wrote me that you were in Europe this summer. Are you not coming to Berlin? I am so anxious to see you again. I have been away from here almost all summer, first for an automobile tour through the Schwartzwald and Tyrol, after, for a long time in Italy.

Now I am back here and returning to my work.

What a pleasure it would be for me to welcome you in Berlin. I cannot imagine that you would be in Germany without sending me a line, or without coming to this city.

Not knowing your European address, I must send this letter to you by way of America and am sorry for the long time it will require to reach you.

*I hope you and all your family will be in good
health.*

> *With greetings to all, and kind love to yourself
> always yours,
> Adele aus der Ohe*[253]

I hope they were able to reunite that summer in Germany. It was to be for the last time, for aus der Ohe was no longer traveling to America and Helena Gilder died five years later, in 1916.

As the years slid by, 1911, 1912, 1913, neither aus der Ohe nor most others could possibly imagine the misery and suffering all of Europe was careening toward, when suddenly in 1914, World War I erupted—a political and economic tragedy of an unprecedented scale. It wreaked havoc on her life and the lives of millions of Europeans.

Berlin was the most densely populated city in the world in 1914. It had grown from a population of less than one million in 1870 to about 2.5 million by 1914.

Adequate food supplies became an issue almost immediately after the outbreak of the war. The two staples of the German diet were bread and potatoes. German soil was not ideal for growing wheat but excellent for rye production. The German government typically exported their rye (primarily to Russia) and imported wheat. There was such confidence that the war would be very brief that, just prior to hostilities breaking out, the government honored their export commitments and shipped most of their rye to Russia. As soon as actual hostilities broke out, England and France blockaded Germany and the anticipated wheat imports never arrived. Bread immediately began to run low and remained scarce for the rest of the war. By the spring of 1915 it was nearly impossible to get bread at all. Due to early frosts and wet conditions the harvests of 1915 and 1916 were poor, and by 1916 potatoes were in short supply as well.

Street riots erupted over the food shortages and also the exorbitant price increases that followed the shortages. Pork and butter became scarce as well as coffee, jam, and sugar.

The winter of 1916–17 was unprecedentedly cold and resulted in genuine famine. This catastrophic "Turnip Winter" (because turnips were about the only food available to most people) truly threatened the health of the Berlin residents. Many people, including women and children, were forced to stand in long lines for hours in the freezing rain to get small bits of food supplies, and "by the fall of 1916, during which time many Berliners worked long hours, ate little of sustaining value, and spent exceeding cold nights in food lines, everyone felt sick."[254] Outbreaks of influenza and tuberculosis were common. Thousands perished in a flu epidemic that broke out in early 1917.

Journalist William Menkel was in Berlin in 1917 and reported,

> The Entente Allies' blockade has kept from Germany much of the food supplies she once imported. Some food articles are undoubtedly very scarce and high priced, and for part of the population entirely unobtainable, while prices generally have gone up ... The new year, as

*far as internal conditions are concerned will be a year
of privation . . . Economy in coal consumption has been
obtained by the early closing of shops and cafes, and
curtailing streetcar and subway service . . . Mr. Herbert
Bayard Swope was in Germany for three months in
the latter part of 1916 as a correspondent of the New
York World. "Life in Germany" says Mr. Swope, "is not
pleasant today. There is a hopeless prison atmosphere
about it that causes men to crack under the strain. Berlin has become a nest of intrigue and gossip. A motive is
looked for behind every man's act.* [255]

Nearly all food supplies were under government control
and were rationed; bread, butter, meats, potatoes, sugar,
milk, cream, eggs, etc. One needed ration cards to make
purchases and could only buy predetermined quantities
based on the size of one's family. Each person was allotted
one egg per week. Meat was allowed five days a week and the
allotment per person was seventy-five grams, which is less
than a quarter of a pound (the equivalent of a rather small
hamburger); and this was not per meal, this was per day.
On Tuesday and Friday, when you could not have meat, you
were allowed to have butter. The bread cards had little tabs,
each tab allowing for a slice of *"Kreigsbrot"* (war bread)[256] or
two tabs for a roll. Consumers were allowed nine pounds
of potatoes per week (roughly about twelve average-sized
potatoes).

A la carte menus virtually disappeared from restaurants and you simply had to accept what the restaurant
gave you. Mass feeding halls were established in the major

German cities in an effort to more efficiently and equitably distribute what meager food supplies were available.

> *Dr. von Heydebrand, the Conservative leader in a speech before the Prussian Diet, said: "Our economic situation is rich in deprivations and sacrifices . . . The town populations are suffering grievously. It is sad to see how long women have to wait for a couple of potatoes and how, for the simplest of necessaries, town dwellers must pay absolutely exorbitant prices . . .* [257]

From April 1917 through January 1918, street protests in Berlin became common and increasingly violent. By the war's end in November 1918, Kaiser Wilhelm II was forced to abdicate and fled the country and there was open fighting in the streets for control of the government. Curfews were imposed and people feared for their lives when leaving their homes.

By the end of the war, aus der Ohe was not only without family, aging, and weakened from lack of proper nutrition, but was also suffering much from a painful and debilitating arthritis that was to plague her for the rest of her life. Her handwriting from this time is greatly deteriorated and it is clear that she is writing with much effort. She also began to have difficulty with her eyesight and there is an increasing largeness to her handwriting.

Despite the hardships of the war and her physical frailty, she remained, like her great teacher, Liszt, keenly interested in the music of the day. A 1920 letter to a Professor Sternke:

LIVING CONDITIONS IN GERMANY AND AUSTRIA 159

DISTRIBUTING FOOD FROM A MILITARY KITCHEN TO THE PEOPLE IN A SUBURB OF BERLIN

the wealthy. Rich and poor fare alike. All get the same quantity and get it at the same time and at the same price. This price restriction applies to the bigger staples, such as bread, fish, certain sorts of meat, and clothing. With money it is possible to buy the finer grades of flour, poultry, cattle and hog meats, and attire, for there are no restraints put about luxuries. The regulations apply only to the necessities. For example, one can buy silk socks in Berlin to-day in such quantities and prices as one wishes, but one must have a police permit, with a careful inquiry preceding its issuance, to buy woolen socks. The same is true of the cheaper grades of clothing, the prices of which have not been much increased.

The greatest food scarcity is in butter, cheese, sugar, cocoa, chocolate, fats, oils, pork, coffee, tea, oranges, lemons, bananas, and eggs. Vegetables are to be had in plenty; also the fruits that Germany raises or that come from her southern allies, such as applies, melons, pears, grapes, and the like.

LIVING BY THE CARD SYSTEM

One must have cards for bread, butter, meat, fruits, potatoes, fats, sugar, milk, cream, and eggs. Meat is allowed five times a week; butter or fats twice a week; eggs, one to each person per week; bread, vegetables, and fish are to be had every day. The bread cards have little tabs on them, each calling for twenty-five grams of *kriegsbrot* (war bread). Each tab is good for a slice of bread or two tabs for a roll. Meat cards

are good for a slice and a half, or 75 grams, of meat. On Tuesdays and Fridays there is no meat to be had, but on these days butter is allotted. Fats for frying can be had on Mondays and Thursdays. Thin-skimmed milk and small particles of saccharine have taken the place of cream and sugar.

Every family is given a card, stating the quantity of food allotted to it, according to its size. These cards are used on stated days at the various markets. Every family has a regular day for purchasing its meat supplies for the week. This regulates the butcher's supply and prevents him being loaded up unnecessarily. He, in turn, is obliged to present his customers' cards to the central governmental supply station when renewing his stock. Game and poultry do not come under the meat restrictions, and can be freely purchased as yet.

Bakers also sell by weekly arrangements. Every consumer is entitled to 1900 grams of baked bread, or 1700 grams of bread and 250 grams of meal or flour. Each consumer is also entitled to 60 grams of butter and 30 grams of oleomargarine. He may also draw 9 pounds of potatoes a week. There is no rule about how these supplies shall be used. A family or an individual can use up all its card rations in a day. For the rest of the week, naturally, they would then have to live on food articles the purchase of which

I hope you still remember me from the Lyceum Club in Berlin, and especially because of the concert with pieces by Felix Gotthelf, whose piano compositions I played then. Now, it is very important to me to continue to promote the compositions of Gotthelf, and I would therefore like to express the request that you would consent to kindly assist me through your considerable influence: a request that I permit myself to express to you, particularly due to the fact that I know that you also esteem Gotthelf's pieces highly. Might it not be possible for you to give me the opportunity to play these two piano numbers by Gotthelf at the Wagner Society in Stettin: "Zur Dämmerstunde" (Three Fantasy Pieces) as well as his Piano Sonata? I would be grateful to you for the sake of the composer, whose work deserves more widespread recognition. Should there be any opportunity to play them, I ask that you would very kindly think of me.[258]

In a note to a Mr. August Weiss, aus der Ohe wrote, "My heartfelt thanks for sending me your compositions, which were forwarded to me here. I won't have time to look at them here, but hope to do so after I return to Berlin."[259]

Almost nothing is known of either of these composers. Felix Gotthelf was born in Munich and did have several of his compositions published in his lifetime. August Weiss was also German born, in the lovely town of Deidesheim in southern Germany, and also had some things published; however, it is very possible that the scores aus der Ohe was referring to were original manuscripts, which are often quite difficult to read.

Her American friend Robert Underwood Johnson had published, many years earlier, a book of poetry entitled *The Winter Hour*,[260] which included these lines:

Ah, who shall wake the charm that lies
Past what is written for the eyes
In such a scroll? The poet's need
Is that a poet's heart should read.
Happy the winter hour and fleet
When flame and waiting passion meet
In her pure fire whose chords betray
The St. Cecilia of our day!
Oh, velvet of that Saxon hand
So lately iron to command!
Like, at the shower's sudden stop,
The softness of the clinging drop.
What tender notes the trance prolong
Of that famed rhythmic cradle-song!
How faery is her woven spell
Of minuet or tarantelle!
Who would return to earth when she
Transports us with a rhapsody!
And when in some symphonic burst
Of joy her spirit is immersed,
That path celestial fain to share,
We vow to breathe but noble air!

Mr. Johnson had given a copy of this book to aus der Ohe. "Many thanks for your book—which gives me perfect delight—I read pages 20 and 21 and had a feeling of sincere pleasure mixed with pride, thinking that the remembrance of my art crossed your mind when you wrote those beautiful lines."[261]

Now this loyal, longtime friend did what he could to help.

To the Editor of the New York Times:

I am sure that across the intervening years the elder generation of American music lovers have not forgotten the distinguished pianist Fräulein Adele aus der Ohe, whose work as a young woman in recital and in concert was long a charming feature of our American Winters. Particularly memorable was her triumph at the dedication of Carnegie Hall, when she played—I think with the Boston Symphony Orchestra—the concerto of Tchaikovsky, winning the tumultuous applause of a picked audience. She was, and presumably still is, Court Pianist at Weimar, though she is living in Berlin—13 [sic] Pariser-Strasse—having with difficulty survived the trying vicissitudes of the war. She is, however no longer equal to the demands of a concert tour, but is chiefly occupied with giving lessons. She is very desirous to have more American pupils at her home, and this note is written in the hope of furthering that desire. Perhaps no one now living so truly represents the Liszt tradition in the piano, for she was indeed the favorite pupil of that master. I cannot think of any better fortune that could befall an advanced student of music than association with so distinguished an artist. I should willingly do anything possible to pro-

mote a relationship of such manifest advantage both to
teacher and to pupil.

    Robert Underwood Johnson[262]

Aus der Ohe began to teach after her return to Berlin in
1906. She had an opportunity to discuss her teaching con-
cepts when Harriette Brower interviewed her in 1913. Ms.
Brower (1854–1928), a pianist, piano teacher, and eventually a journalist, was one of the first Americans to write
about piano technique, the mechanics of piano playing.
Her writings first appeared in various musical magazines
and proved to be so popular that in 1911 she published her
first book, *The Art of the Pianist.* (She eventually published a
total of ten books.) Her acclaimed three-volume interview
series,[263] *Piano Mastery* (1915), *Piano Mastery, Second Series*
(1917), and *Modern Masters of the Keyboard* (1926), consisted
of interviews of nearly every great pianist alive. Most of the
interviews centered around some aspect of piano teaching
or technique. In preparation for the first volume, Harriette
Brower traveled to Europe to interview various European-
based pianists, including Adele aus der Ohe.

My time is divided between playing in concert, compos-
ing and my own studies. I give almost no lessons, for I
have not time for them. I never have more than a couple
of pupils studying with me at one time; they must be
both talented and eager. The amount of time I consider
necessary for practice depends, of course, on quickness
of comprehension. In general, I may say four, or at
most, five hours are quite sufficient, if used with abso-

lute concentration. The quality of practice is the great essential. If the passage under consideration is not understood, a thousand times going over it will be only vain repetitions; therefore, understand the construction and meaning of the passage in the beginning, and then a thousand repetitions ought to make it perfect. There is so much practice which can be done away from the instrument, by reading the notes from the printed page and thinking about them. Is this understood in America? Always listen to your playing, to every note you make on the piano; I consider this point of the very first importance. My pupils are generally well advanced or are those who intend making music a profession. I have, however, occasionally taken a beginner. This point of listening to every note, of training the ear, should stand at the very foundation. In regard to hand position, I endeavor not to be narrow and pedantic. If pupils play with good tone and can make reasonably good effects, I take them at the point where they are and try to bring them forward, even if the hand position is not just what I would like. If I stop everything and let them do nothing but hand position, they will be discouraged and think they are beginning all over again. This beginning again is sometimes detrimental. To take a pupil at his present point, and carry him along was also Liszt's idea. He did not like to change a hand position to which the player has grown accustomed for one which seems unnatural, and which the pianist has to work a long time to acquire. He felt that one's time could be spent to more advantage. There are so many

legitimate positions, each hand is a separate study,
and is apt to take the position most natural to itself.[264]

Very little would be known of aus der Ohe's teaching were it not for an amazingly talented and intrepid woman from Brinsmade, North Dakota—a town so small it probably never had a population of more than several hundred people. Alma Mehus,[265] at the age of twenty, made her way to Berlin and became a student of aus der Ohe. She had previously studied with Josef Lhevinne at the American Conservatory in Chicago. (Her sister, Belle Mehus, traveled to Berlin in the summer of 1930 to also study with aus der Ohe.)

I arrived in Berlin in the spring of 1923. It was the cultural center of the world at that time, and I immediately fell in love with the city. When I arrived I did not know exactly with whom I would study piano. I met many interesting people, among whom was Mrs. Artur Abell. She was the wife of the Berlin representative for the Musical Courier, and a very well respected person in the musical circles in Berlin. It was she who introduced me to Adele aus der Ohe and I am eternally grateful for that introduction.

It did not take long for me to realize that in aus der Ohe I had found a great teacher. I said to her once that so much of what she taught me was similar to that of my former teacher Josef Lhevinne. Her response was "We [pianists] often come to the same conclusions."

I never heard aus der Ohe in a large concert hall— she had already retired from public playing. She did on occasion invite a small group of friends to her home and play for them and I was invited to some of these soirees. I remember her playing as marvelous. Particularly vivid in my memory is the last Sonata of Schubert. She played it so beautifully. I remember her also playing the Liszt transcription of the "Liebestod" from Wagner's Tristan and Isolde. At the end, she closed the piano and would play no more. I later asked why and she said, "After that music there is nothing more to say." Her technique was flawless and she had a big beautiful sound. At the great climaxes the sound just came out bigger and bigger.

Aus der Ohe spoke perfect English but on occasion there would not be an appropriate phrase for what she wanted to say so she would revert to German. I often think of those German phrases she would use. For example, she would say to "immer ausspielen." She meant that one should always play all of the notes. That is not to say that they are all equally important, but they should all be played.

In my piano lessons with aus der Ohe I never did any technical exercises. Technique was discussed only within the context of whatever particular piece of music I might be studying at the time. In a letter she sent me, she made some comments on practicing.

My dear Miss Mehus:

Your letter interested me very much, all that you say about your work. Brahms-Paganini, as well as

Brahms-Handel, are both as splendid for technique as for repertoire. It takes a time to get them ripe for concert, therefore the sooner you begin with them the better. It would be good to take up the more difficult numbers of Brahms-Handel even if not the whole work as yet. But think always of your hands and don't overwork. Remember Liszt's advise: "One must work until it tires, but then no longer!" "Man darf es nicht forcieren." [One must not force it.] Change is a good rest too; for instance if you have worked hard on technical problems, take for a change easy things that will be useful as studies in tone coloring, phrasing, and interpretation . . .[266]

I worked on the Cello Etude [Op. 25 No. 7] of Chopin with aus der Ohe and she showed me a spot in one of the cadenzas where she said, "Liszt did it that way but I have found it is better to do it this way." I was thunderstruck to hear her say that but she was so sincere and conscientious about her work that I have no doubt her way was better than Liszt's.

She made some interesting comments about repertoire. She said that one should know everything but that one need not play everything. She felt one should play in public only those things one does very well but that one should know a great deal more than just one's own repertoire. Sometimes I jokingly wish she hadn't said that because there is so terribly much music to know!

Perhaps one of the greatest events in my life occurred while I was in Berlin, studying with Adele aus der Ohe. I received an invitation to play with the Berlin Philharmonic. I wrote to aus der Ohe (she was in Italy at the time) to ask her if she thought I should accept the offer. She wrote back immediately:

_____

My dear Miss Mehus:

Late at night I received your letter by express. Of course, you can very well play in March one of the Concertos or all three. I advise principally the Tchaikovsky, but I have no doubt that also Liszt and Schumann will be quite ready for a good public performance by that time. You may also work up the Grieg, which is very grateful, and not difficult. While Beethoven and Schumann require more time to ripen into perfection than the Grieg—So, by all means, do accept the engagement as soloist for the concerts mentioned in your letter. Never refuse anything of the sort, for it helps much to your development as artist. For to play in public is also a thing that will be practiced. So work as hard and as conscientious as you can. And go ahead with good courage. It might be good for your technique to study between the concertos the Brahms-Paganini Variations; and for working up a solo repertoire: the Chopin Fantasy and Barcarolle . . . Prepare all, also all Chopin Etudes Op. 25 and posthumous . . . It goes quicker when you have all prepared. [267]

(As a postscript to this story—at one of my very first lessons aus der Ohe asked me which concertos I had studied, and I confessed that I had not studied any. She

said that we can easily correct that and that I should
begin the Tchaikovsky B-flat minor, the Liszt E-flat, and
the Schumann. Quite an assignment for one lesson!)

One incident that has remained in my memory occurred
just before I was to play with the Berlin Philharmonic.
I went to hear Gieseking play a recital. One of the
pieces was the Kreisleriana of Schumann and after he
had played the first page or so he must have forgotten
because he stopped and began again. Of course the
second time went perfectly but I couldn't help thinking
that if that can happen to Gieseking what will happen
to me when I play with orchestra! I just kept my mind
on what I was to do and aus der Ohe had instilled such
confidence in me that I felt if aus der Ohe thinks I know
it, I must know it!

Aus der Ohe wanted me to be prepared for anything
that might happen and she had me learn the orchestral
score as well as my own part. She told me what had
happened to her on one occasion when she was playing
the Tchaikovsky Concerto. There is a spot where the
time changes and the horns need to make an entrance.
The conductor failed to bring them in and aus der Ohe
started to play the horn part on the piano. The conductor happened to be none other than Artur Nikisch. Aus
der Ohe had a good sense of humor and this amused
her. She said that when Nikisch realized that what he
was hearing on the piano should have been in the horn
section, the back of his neck turned red! Aus der Ohe

showed me things that she did a little differently in the concerto and then she said to me, "Now you don't have to tell this to anyone. If they want to know, tell them to come and hear you."

An example of aus der Ohe's phenomenal memory is shown in a letter she sent me:

"As to the Brahms-Handel Variations, I find one should always play them all and with all repetitions, as marked. Most of the great artists whom I heard do so. Still there is no rule without exceptions. When I heard them played in New York by Paderewski, I noticed that he omitted the 16, 17, 18, 19th, and 21st variations. Another artist repeated them all with the exception of 23 and 24 which he does not repeat on account of their great likeness. So you see opinions, like tastes, are different and you must think of it and act according to your own judgment, but may your judgment always be for the highest standards and highest ideals."[268]

When aus der Ohe wrote that letter, she probably had not looked at the score for years and it was certainly many years since she had heard those pianists play but she was able to remember those things exactly.

By the summer of 1923, as Alma Mehus was arriving each week at 6 Pariser Strasse for those piano lessons that she would cherish for the rest of her life, Germany was in the midst of one of the most spectacular economic meltdowns ever known. At the most fevered moment of this hyperinflation the exchange rate topped one trillion marks to one U.S. dollar, and a newspaper that sold for one mark in May 1922 sold for seventy million marks by November 1923.

How did this catastrophe happen?

Germany had assumed the war would be brief and the government chose to finance it through borrowing rather than taxation and savings. As the war dragged on, the government continued borrowing more and more and prices began to rise as a result. Still, everyone thought that once the war ended the economy would return to normal pre-war conditions. However, at the conclusion of the war, in addition to the enormous debt load that had accrued over four long years of fighting, the Treaty of Versailles imposed crushing war reparations on the German people, amounts that were impossible to pay.

Even though World War I officially ended on November 11, 1918, for the German people that date was simply one more on the calendar. The years following the signing of the armistice were ones of endless suffering.

Financially, for nearly four years, the ultimate cata-clysm was always just round the corner. It always arrived, and there was always an even worse one on its way—again, and again, and again. The speeches, the newspaper articles, the official records, the diplomatic telegrams, the letters and diaries of the period, all report month by month, year by year, that things could not go on like that any longer: and yet things always did, from bad to worse, to worse, to worse. It was unimaginable in 1921 that 1922 could hold more terrors. They came,

*sure enough, and were in turn eclipsed, and more than
eclipsed, with the turn of the year.*[269]

The nation was bankrupt and it seemed the only way
to cope was an endless circle of raising prices and then
printing more money to allow people to pay the exorbitant
prices. Between 1913 and 1921 the price of rye bread had
risen by thirteen times, and beef by seventeen; and these
were the "more modest" price increases! Sugar, milk,
pork, and even potatoes had risen by more than twenty-
five times the prewar prices. Prices began to be published
in the newspapers each morning: Tramway fare—50,000
marks, Auto Taxi—600,000 marks.

The great German pianist "Artur Schnabel gave a concert and received his fee in a suitcase full of bills. "I had to
ask a man to help carry my fee home," he said later. "On my
way home, I passed a delicatessen and to relieve my helper
I spent half my fee on a couple of sausages. The next morning I saw in the paper that I could not even get one sausage
for the other half of my fee."[270]

Shoppers routinely packed suitcases full of money
prior to heading out to buy a few essentials and thieves
would occasionally steal these suitcases, dumping out the
money and leaving it behind lying in the street. Customers
at restaurants negotiated prices in advance because prices
could change before the meal was served. Women used
money to light fires in their stoves to cook the morning
coffee; it was cheaper and easier to burn the money than to
try to use it to obtain a bit of precious fuel. The stories were
nearly unbelievable, almost as if the people were caught up

in some dark comedy and at any moment everyone would suddenly burst into laughter at the absurdity of it all.

Workers endlessly protested that wages were not keeping up and there were frequent strikes. Berliners became used to the disruptions. Electricity was shut off, railway service was interrupted, and even Berlin's city water supply was cut off at one point. When Germany was unable to meet its war reparation payments, in lieu of cash the French army marched into the Ruhr Valley and took control of Germany's coal supply, thus eliminating, among many other things, fuel for home heating.

The children suffered greatly. "All children of every class, according to a study in the *Frankfort-on-the-Main* were two years physically and mentally backward for their ages."[271] Another study for 1922 noted that "nearly 25 percent of the children leaving school were below the normal spread of weights and heights and 30 percent were unfit to work for reasons of health."[272]

Louis Lochner arrived in Berlin during this period and eventually became bureau chief for the Associated Press. "I visited a typical Youth Welfare Station," he said later. "Children who looked as though they were eight or nine years old proved to be thirteen. I learned that there were then 15,000 tubercular children in Berlin, that 23 percent of the children examined by the city health authorities were badly undernourished."[273]

The old were equally helpless. "One elderly writer, Maximilian Bern, withdrew all his savings, more than 100,000 marks, and spent them on a subway ticket. He took a ride around Berlin and then locked himself in his apartment and starved to death."[274] People redeemed investments that had amassed over a lifetime and felt fortunate if their accumulated funds bought one loaf of bread.

"Throughout the cities, lack of food, clothing, and warmth had produced all their concomitant ailments, from ulcers to rickets, from pneumonia to tuberculosis, all pitifully aggravated by the soaring costs of medicine and medical supplies."[275] If one became sick, one simply waited it out and either got better or got worse. Some, out of sheer desperation, went to Catholic convents where they could at least receive some basic nursing charitably.

Petty crime became rampant. Metal plaques on national monuments had to be removed for safe keeping, brass plates were stolen from front doors of homes, lead disappeared from roofs, and gas was siphoned from cars. People used anything to barter until they could get what they needed. With a piece of the family china you might barter for a shirt, which you then might barter for some potatoes, which could then keep your family alive one more day.

Berlin became practically amoral. Prostitutes of both sexes roamed the streets and cocaine use was widespread. By 1923 Berlin was like a city under siege and for weeks at a time practically all supplies of meat, eggs, and vegetables to the capital were stopped. People literally starved in the streets. Whenever an emaciated, malnourished horse dropped dead, a horde of people suddenly appeared to butcher it and cart off the precious meat.[276]

The price increases were astronomical. A loaf of bread that cost the already enormous amount of 163 marks in 1922 cost 1,500,000 marks by September 1923, and two months later cost 200,000,000,000 marks. A postage stamp that sold for four marks in 1920 sold for 50,000,000,000 marks in 1923. One U.S. dollar was equal to 100 billion marks. The numbers were simply dizzying; people could hardly comprehend these fantastic amounts.

In this unbelievable atmosphere of desperation and frustration, people would gather at the Reichsbank in Berlin, eager to grab bundles of money as quickly as they came off the press. "Day and night thirty paper mills, 150 printing firms, and 2,000 printing presses toiled away, adding perpetually to the blizzard of banknotes under which the country's economy had already disappeared."[277]

Aus der Ohe spent part of 1923 in Italy and Alma Mehus remembered,

She was a friend of the Countess von Hindenburg and the countess had a home in Italy so aus der Ohe went as her house guest. Because of the severity of the financial and political situation in Germany I had difficulty getting to Italy. I bought my train ticket in Berlin and I think it cost something like a billion marks, the inflation was that bad. I also had to buy a ticket for my luggage and that cost me almost as much as my ticket. We got as far as Munich but there the train was stopped and we were told that we could go no farther. There had been some uprising and the Bavarian border was closed. We had no choice but to go back to Berlin and start out all over again. I had to buy another ticket but the second time the train got through.

A letter that aus der Ohe wrote me in 1923, before I went to Italy, indicates how much the situation in Germany saddened her. We had previously discussed the possibility of spending the winter together in Vienna.

My dear Miss Mehus:

Whether I can come to Vienna is still uncertain. I have no idea how prices and circumstances are there. Should you go there do write me as much about it as you can to the above Italian address should I not see you anymore at Berlin.

I return, if God will, in November, date soon to be fixed.

It is lovely here, also a good place to work. I enjoy climate and friends. But the terrible uncertainty, how it is there in Germany, how my friends are there, reduces much the pleasure for me. Away from my house I suffer much with those I love there and this makes me feel that I would rather remain at Berlin than go to Vienna . . .[278]

"People just didn't understand what was happening. All the economic theory they had been taught didn't provide for the phenomenon . . . when the 1,000 billion mark note came out, few bothered to collect the change when they spent it. By November 1923, with one dollar equal to one trillion marks, the breakdown was complete."[279] "The German experience with hyperinflation was the most spectacular the world had seen."[280]

According to one historian, Alan Bullock, "It [the

hyperinflation] had the effect, which is the unique quality of economic catastrophe, of reaching down to and touching every single member of the community in a way which no political event can. The savings of the middle classes were wiped out at a single blow with the ruthlessness which no revolution could ever equal."[281]

What happened next is as amazing as the Great Inflation itself. The tornado of the inflation was succeeded by the "miracle" of the Rentenmark.[282] Nine zeros were struck from the currency so that one Rentenmark was equal to one billion old marks. In many ways this was simply trading one piece of paper for another. The Rentenmark was not backed by gold but rather by mortgages, but the German people desperately wanted to believe that reform had arrived, and so they did!

But although the country functioned again, the savings were never restored. Widows dependent on insurance found themselves destitute. People who had worked a lifetime found that their pensions would not buy one cup of coffee.

Pearl Buck, the American writer who became famous for her novels of China, was in Germany in 1923. She wrote later, "The cities were still there, the houses not bombed and in ruins, but the victims were millions of people. They had lost their fortunes, their savings; they were dazed and inflation-shocked and did not understand how it had happened to them and who the foe was who had defeated them. Yet they had lost their self-assurance, their feeling that they themselves could be the masters of their own lives if only they worked hard enough..."[283]

A wrenching description of aus der Ohe's life comes

from Matthew Josephson, an American journalist living in Berlin in 1922 and 1923.

> ...*my earnings of thirty dollars a week definitely placed me in the millionaire class... The mark had dropped from a value of two hundred to five hundred to the dollar shortly after our arrival, then had fallen to one thousand, and recently to three thousand marks per dollar... The case of my wife's piano teacher illustrated the plight of a large part of the German middle class. She was none other than Adele aus der Ohe, one of the world-famous pianists of the nineteenth century. Fräulein aus der Ohe, a tall, dignified spinster of fifty-nine had been a pupil of Liszt and a friend of Clara Schumann, Brahms, and Tchaikovsky... Now the large fortune she had accumulated during a lifetime of giving concerts before millions of people was all gone, for it had been loyally invested in government war bonds all made worthless by inflation. She subsisted half-famished in her once luxurious, now musty, apartment, surrounded by the memorabilia of her public career; and survived only because her two servants whom she could no longer pay, retained their lodgings in her place while going out to work elsewhere, yet with beautiful devotion brought in a little food each day which they shared with her.*
>
> *Fräulein aus der Ohe knew nothing of the kind of world in which she was living. She was an exceedingly proud and high-minded woman; when my wife kept raising her fee (because of the fall of the mark), leaving*

*her increasingly large bundles of paper money, the old
lady could make nothing of it and would not even look
at the money left for her.*

*One evening we invited her to dinner and fed her
red meat and Burgundy. She seemed so weak and
crippled by arthritis that we wondered if she would
be able to play for us. But after eating and drinking,
she marched, with flushed face, to the piano and performed Schubert's "Wanderer Phantasie" as we had
never heard it played before, or since...[284]*

The servants Mr. Josephson referred to were Herr and
Frau Meischner, and it is heartwarming to know of these
lovely people and to know that aus der Ohe was not completely alone in her final years. Family had been such an
incredibly important aspect of aus der Ohe's life and now
she had these people as her surrogate family, for they were
indeed a family; the Meischners had two small children, a
daughter and a son, who brightened everyone's lives. The
little girl was a fine musician and aus der Ohe gave her
piano lessons. The amazing love and devotion these people
felt for aus der Ohe is revealed by their little daughter's
name—she was Adele also, Adele Meischner.

Adele (Adleheit) had been a beloved family name
for the Ohe's for generations. It was the name of aus der
Ohe's own grandmother and now she had a small girl to
dote on and who would carry forward this beautiful and
cherished name. One gets a sense of the warm grandmo-
therly feelings aus der Ohe had for these children from a
letter to her student, Alma Mehus. "The Meischners send

you their greetings. Little Adelchen made great progress in her music. Her gifts are marvelous. She and I gave a Konzert together on November 11 at Berlin (Lyceum Club). Adelchen played alone some of her own compositions, besides works by Mozart, Beethoven, and Bach. We played at four hands together, Schubert and Beethoven. And I alone played Ebel, aus der Ohe, and Schubert. There was a large, fine and enthusiastic audience. Heiny and Adelchen go now to school. They both send you their love. All of us send you our best wishes for a merry Christmas and a very happy New Year."[285] "I am glad you liked little Adele's *Waldesrauschen*. She composed a great deal; and anyway is a wonderfully gifted child, and a sweet child too."[286]

Throughout these tumultuous years aus der Ohe remained in contact with her student, Alma, for whom she had such respect.

Your letter gave me a great deal of pleasure. I congratulate you for your success on the 11th, of which I also heard from another side. May it help you in your artistic career. The concert at Amsterdam of which the Concertmeister spoke, you should certainly give, if possible. Do not refuse any opportunity that offers itself.[287]

Alma recalled, "After I played my Chicago debut I wrote to tell her about it."

My dear Alma
Long ago I was going to write to you and only today I am doing it. You know how life is going here and there-

fore you will understand my apparent laziness, which is not laziness but a want of time. I was so interested in all you wrote and am now anxious to hear how you are getting along in your playing and career. Your programs were fine and your Chicago criticisms a great encouragement. I have no doubt that you ought to succeed in your career. At first things often go slow but one ought not to be discouraged. I have made the observation that quick successes often die out. I know of a number of cases where this came true. Do always practice with care and attention, do always play with enthusiasm. Try to always be at your best, whether alone, whether before a few or before thousands. Make playing at your best the rule and you will have it at your command when it is important. I know artists who cannot play well when the audience is small. This seemed to me always inartistic. Why should the few who came suffer for those who stayed away? Of course we need money in order to live and the audiences to make money, if possible, but the inspiration for playing should never come from the audience alone but from the art itself by the divine gift bestowed upon a few . . .[288]

Berlin was a city of about 2.5 million people at the start of the war. By the 1920s the population of Berlin soared to four million people. Russian émigrés, fleeing the violence of their own revolution, arrived in Berlin in droves—ballerina Anna Pavlova, opera basso Boris Chaliapin, artist Wassily Kandinsky, impresario Sol Hurok, pianist Vladimir Horowitz, writer Maxim Gorki—all came to Berlin.

Jobs were scarce and one of the greatest cellists ever, nineteen-year-old Gregor Piatigorsky, "found himself sleeping on a bench in the Tiergarten, storing his cello under the bench and hoping that the police would understand. One night it rained and Piatigorsky took refuge in the men's room of the zoo station. When the rain finally stopped he was so depressed by the idea of returning to his bench in the park that he headed instead for the nearby Philharmonic Hall. Carrying his cello like a badge of office, he marched through the stage entrance, and sneaked into the hall in time to hear the great Busoni conduct Beethoven's Eighth Symphony.

"After the concert," Piatigorsky recalled later, "I took my cello without being questioned by anyone. As I was about to step out of the building, the icy wind stopped me and I turned back. My shirt and socks were damp and I was miserably cold... The last people were leaving. A little later the doors were locked and there was complete darkness. The silence and emptiness of the huge building were ghastly. For a long time I stood still, my heart pounding. I felt trapped and wanted to cry for help... I saw a door leading to a loge... Soon I was undressed and settled for the night. How warm and comfortable it [was] here, and what an improvement over the bench of the Tiergarten... I was ready to fall asleep, but... a sudden irresistible urge to play seized me. I got up, grabbed my cello, and naked as I was, moved toward the stage. I could not find the stairs leading to it, so I climbed onto it from the hall... and began to play. The sound of the cello, eerie yet humanly

*full-throated came back to me from the dark immensity
of the great hall. Held fast by this unique experience, I
played to the limits of my endurance. Exhausted but
elated, I finally returned to the loge. In the morning, I
was awakened by the orchestra playing a Schumann
symphony. I thought it rather nice to rest on the couch
there unseen, and enjoy the fine music in the morning . . . The orchestra was still rehearsing when I walked
out of the building."*[289]

Yet gradually, almost miraculously, out of these ashes
of war and economic catastrophe, a Phoenix arose—the arts
began to flourish. Dadaism, a cultural movement meant to
ridicule what its participants considered to be the mean-
inglessness of the modern world, transformed philosophy.
The Bauhaus movement revolutionized architecture. Albert
Einstein, one of the most brilliant minds of the twentieth
century, was busily revolutionizing science, oblivious to the
political and economic turmoil all around him.

The young pianist Rudolph Serkin arrived in Berlin
to study with Busoni. "[Busoni] said I shouldn't have any
lessons. I was seventeen and he said that was old enough
for me to have a style of my own. He said I should go to lots
of concerts and if I liked one, I would learn something. And
if I didn't like one, maybe I would also learn something . . . I
gave a concert myself, at the Singakademie. There were
only twenty people in the audience, but among them were
Busoni, Schnabel, and Einstein . . ."[290]

Pianists Claudio Arrau and Wilhelm Backhaus, along
with Horowitz, Serkin, and Schnabel, all lived in Berlin.

Erich Kleiber directed the Berlin State Opera, Bruno Walter the Municipal Opera, and Otto Klemperer the Kroll
Opera, located in the Tiergarten. When aus der Ohe's old
friend and musical collaborator from their Boston days,
Artur Nikisch died in 1922, Wilhelm Furtwängler took over
his post at the Berlin Philharmonic.

Arnold Schoenberg was developing his twelve tone
theories, which dictated that a composer use all twelve
tones of the chromatic scale and no tone could be repeated
until all other eleven had been used. Schoenberg's pupil,
Alban Berg, composed his great opera *Wozzeck*, which no
one would publish or produce. Berg finally published it
himself, thus creating a mountain of unsalable paper!
Kleiber heard a piano version of it in 1924 and decided to
give the premiere at the Berlin State Opera, "even if it costs
me my job!" At the opening night on December 14, 1925,
the audience reacted violently. "There were fist fights,"
said Hans Heinsheimer, who was there, "angry challenges
shouted across the orchestra seats and from the boxes,
deriding laughter, boos, and hostile whistles that threatened for some time to overpower the small but, at last,
vigorous group of believers. As the tall noble figure of the
composer appeared before the curtain, the riots increased,
the bravos and boos, the waves of enthusiastic excitement
and outraged hostility. Berg seemed a little taken aback by
it, perhaps a shade paler that usual, but was quite unaffected, calm, very sure of his work."[291]

Thirteen-year-old Yehudi Menuhin made his Berlin
debut in 1929, playing the concerti of Bach, Beethoven,
and Brahms. After the concert the fifty-year-old Albert

Einstein rushed backstage saying, "Today, Yehudi you have once again proved to me that there is a God in heaven."[292]

In 1927, upon the one hundredth anniversary of the death of Beethoven, Arthur Schnabel became one of the first pianists to perform all thirty-two of Beethoven's Piano Sonatas in concert. He performed them in a series of seven consecutive Sundays and, in his characteristic dislike of display, played them at the *Volksbühne* [People's Theatre] in Berlin's working class district. Two thousand people gathered Sunday after Sunday to hear this monumental achievement.

Might there have been, somewhere in that crowd of two thousand, a tall elderly woman, most likely dressed in black, walking feebly from arthritic joints, but listening intently? Possibly some of the older audience members still remembered her and whispered with awe, "It's aus der Ohe!" as she entered the hall. Possibly some even greeted her as she made her way to her seat and she would have politely nodded and smiled. It is, of course, all conjecture, but Beethoven sonatas had been such an integral part of aus der Ohe's concert repertoire. This feat of performing all of them would surely have been of interest to her.

Despite increasing physical frailties, aus der Ohe remained in contact with her friends, writing amazingly positive letters of encouragement and hope in spite of the enormous difficulties in her own life.

> *My dear Alma:*
> *I was so glad to get your letter. Everything you wrote was*
> *extremely interesting to me . . . I have been very busy, so*

much so that I have almost no time for writing letters.
So you must pardon me for not having written sooner.
I have been thinking of you a great deal, wishing with
all my heart for your success. Don't get discouraged if
things seem to go slowlyer [sic] than you wish. Only
persevere always in striving towards perfection and
success is sure to come, for I had always the impression
that you have the qualities that promise success.

> *With love—*
> *always yours,*
> *Adele aus der Ohe*[293]

Alma recalled "Aus der Ohe was a really noble person. She had such poise and courage. She was not only a great artist but also a great person. She seemed to have such a deep understanding of matters. Also she was quite religious and believed in reincarnation. I remember several religious paintings in her apartment."

It was in a half-whispered voice, with tear-filled eyes and trembling hands, that Alma read aloud this beautiful final letter from her great teacher. Even after fifty years the emotions were visceral: "It is very precious to me."

October 11th, 1931
Dearest Alma:
I'm not quite sure whether I replied to your letter (writ-
ten to me in December) or not—at any rate I feel a long-
ing to write to you and to inquire how your concerts in
February came off. I hope they were successful. I have
a great belief in your artistic possibilities for there is so

much music in you, so much power of interpretation that you cannot help being successful if you keep before the public.

If God has given a gift there is also a place for it in this world.

Your friend

Adele aus der Ohe

Courtesy of David Cannata and Rena Charnin Mueller

Rachmaninoff

Aus der Ohe fled back to Europe just at a time when many were beginning to sense a need to flee to America. She went home to mourn the death of her sister and became mired in one of the worst upheavals of all time. By 1928 she was old, ill, without family, and destitute. She had survived World War I and the Great Inflation that followed, but her time had run out.

A disciple of numerology might quickly conclude that increments of four were extremely unlucky for aus der Ohe. In 1902 her brother Gustav died; in 1906 Mathilde died; in 1910 her sister Fernande died; in 1914 Germany went to war and she was trapped in Berlin. The war lasted four years until 1918, and then in 1922 the Great Inflation wiped out her life savings. This was tragedy of almost biblical proportions. To start over was impossible.

Had she stayed in America, she most likely would have continued concertizing many more years, and then possibly moved on to a prestigious teaching position. Had she made America her permanent home, she most likely would have transferred her investments and enjoyed a retirement free of financial worries.

Possibly a wonderful biography would have been written and her personal papers preserved. She had letters from Liszt, Tchaikovsky, Brahms, Clara Schumann, and so many of the famous musicians of her day. Her scores might have been preserved, and her later compositions published. Also, little did she (or anyone else) know what technological marvels lay just around the corner.

Piano rolls were the first means of preserving a piano performance for later reproduction by way of a self-playing piano in one's home. It was a system where a roll of paper had holes punched in it, each hole representing a key on the piano. As this was unrolled (via a foot pedal) it passed over a bar, causing the various notes to sound on the keyboard. These became very popular about 1900 and lasted until around 1925. Many great pianists had performances preserved for posterity using this method.

Thomas Edison had invented the phonograph already in 1877 but it was only about 1900 that it became practical to record musical performances and, by the 1920s, recordings were already commonplace. Also around 1900, moving pictures were becoming practical and by the 1920s the Hollywood movie industry was well underway. Movies with sound, "talkies," were developed by the late 1920s. All of these technological advances were well within aus der Ohe's life span, and many of her contemporaries left performances for our enjoyment and erudition through these various methods of preserving sound. What a treasure it would be to have a sampling of her legendary Liszt playing.

But all this was happening in wealthy America, not in impoverished and war-torn Germany. It is very likely that, had she remained in America, she would be well remembered as the phenomenal artist that she was, instead of falling into nearly complete oblivion, as has been the enormously unfortunate case.

Belle Mehus from Bismarck, North Dakota, was quite possibly aus der Ohe's last student. Belle traveled to Berlin to study with her in the summer of 1930. By this time aus der Ohe was approaching seventy and was in very poor health, yet her mind was alert. Belle described an early lesson:

> One of the first pieces I played for aus der Ohe was a Rhapsody by Dohnanyi. Aus der Ohe liked the way I played it but said she was unfamiliar with the piece and asked if I would leave the music with her. I did, and when I returned the following week for my next lesson she gave it back to me and asked if I was aware that there was a typographical error in the music. She opened the score and showed me exactly which notes had been misprinted and told me what the correct notes should be. She then asked if I would like to hear her play it and she sat at the piano and proceeded to play it perfectly—and from memory. I was astonished that she had worked through the piece so thoroughly in such a short period of time but I came to realize that there was a complete thoroughness about everything she did. She was just incredible.
>
> I arrived at one of my lessons dressed to go to the opera because I would have to go right from my lesson

in order to be on time. When aus der Ohe asked why I was dressed for the evening I said that I was on my way to hear Tristan and Isolde. She said it was her favorite opera so I asked if there was anything I needed to know to prepare myself—since I was hearing the opera for the first time. She said to me, "Oh how I envy you, hearing Tristan and Isolde for the first time. Do absolutely nothing but to go and enjoy it.

News of aus der Ohe's desperate plight reached America and her longtime friends and admirers did what they could.

For the benefit of Adele aus der Ohe, the celebrated pianist and Liszt pupil of a quarter century ago, a concert will be held in the Town Hall on Dec. 23 . . . it is about twenty years since she has been heard in this country. Of late Mme. aus der Ohe has been teaching in Berlin but recently has been too ill to take any pupils. A letter received recently by Hyman Rovinsky[294] told of her illness and suffering . . .[295]

Albert Morris Bagby, her old and dear friend, whom she had first met in Weimar at the 1885 master classes with Liszt, who had so many years ago written the wonderful *Century Magazine* article that introduced her to the American public, and who had so faithfully followed her career over the years, did what he could for his friend.

Since its incorporation four years ago, the Music Lovers' Foundation, Inc. of this city, through voluntary con-

tribution and other methods, has been able to bestow pensions on artists who, in spite of great achievements in the world of music, have found themselves without adequate support in their declining years. Although some of these artists who have been aided had amassed a competence, nothing remains of their affluence, owing to unfortunate investments or in some cases due to the loss of fortunes on account of the World War.

It was through the efforts of the foundation that the late Mme. Minnie Hauk[296] has been aided for several years as well as Miss Adele aus der Ohe, a pianist, who formerly was highly esteemed in New York. Such pensions have not been given as a matter of charity but rather as an appreciation of the high standard attained, taking also into consideration the straightened circumstances of those artists.

In order to continue their efforts to aid unfortunate artists, it has been decided to hold, on March 18, in the ballroom of the Waldorf-Astoria another Musical Morning, under the direction of Albert Morris Bagby, who instituted years ago this form of musical entertainment that has attracted the important members of society during December and January for nearly forty years.[297]

Another who heard of her suffering and responded with kindness was Sergei Rachmaninoff. He was born in Russia in April 1873, into a musical family and began his piano training at an early age. Later he studied with his first cousin, the famous pianist and teacher Alexander (Sasha) Siloti. Siloti himself was born in 1863 and in 1883, at the

age of nineteen, went to Weimar to study with the legendary Franz Liszt. He remained a student until Liszt's death
in July 1886. Siloti had planned to take his talented young
cousin to Weimar, but unfortunately Liszt died before these
plans could be carried out. Rachmaninoff was only thirteen
at the time of Liszt's death.

Rachmaninoff undoubtedly heard many stories about
Siloti's years of study with the great Franz Liszt and undoubtedly stories of the other students as well. Aus der Ohe knew
Siloti well and liked him very much. Rachmaninoff would
have heard stories of her amazing abilities. He moved to
America in 1918, following the Russian Revolution. In early
1928, aware of aus der Ohe's illness and financial difficulties, he sent her a gift of money. She responded with a lovely
thank you.

June 1, 1928

Esteemed Mr. Rachmaninoff:

*It is with my most sincere thanks that I am writing to
you. I cannot thank you enough for the nice present you
sent me—and it is in addition to the donations brought
by my dear Bagby. Your kindness and sweet soul are
legendary, but it is only now that I realize it is true.*

*I have been wanting to write to you for years—
please forgive my hesitancy: for a long time I have
been a big admirer of your music—especially of your
piano concertos that I hold in high esteem. You ought
to be aware that I had the huge honor of playing with
Maestro Tchaikovsky at least four times, the last being
in St. Petersburg for the premiere of his "Symphony*

Pathétique," as soloist for his First Concerto for Piano, a work that is one of the most brilliant of its kind. And at my piano, next to my score of this work, annotated by Tchaikovsky himself, I have copies of your second and third concertos in an edition of merited beauty.[298] If only Tchaikovsky had heard your music! How he would have smiled! This is what Master [Liszt] would have done. You know, Sasha [Siloti] spoke to all of us about you, his young cousin. And how very excited we would have been to see you fulfill your potential under the tutelage of the master! Unfortunately, this never happened. He left us too soon and we miss him every day.

Please accept, Mr. Rachmaninoff, my deep respect and my warmest wishes for your continuing good health, and again many thanks for your generous gift.

Your ever devoted

Adele aus der Ohe

Two years later, Rachmaninoff mailed additional donations and aus der Ohe responded with this second letter:

July 6, 1930

Dear Sergei Vasilych,

Your note has been lying on my desk awaiting a response. However, as you know, the days do not belong to me anymore. It is more my fingers and my hands, and now above all my knees, that need their own schedule. Again and again you offered to help me in my times of need— not only can I no longer play the piano, but now even students are beyond my strength. Life is far from easy in

Berlin now, but I am better here than anywhere else in Germany. When I received your letter by special delivery from the Russicher Musikverlag,[299] *I was moved to tears. Again, thank you for your help, thank you, thank you. You ask me about the years in Weimar, the years that you yourself nearly benefitted from, and indeed, Sasha must have told you the stories about The Master and his children. But this season of change is not pleasant, and I will soon write to you of the golden age.*

 Your ever devoted,

 Adele aus der Ohe

By this time aus der Ohe's physical condition was dreadful and she was suffering greatly. Not only had the arthritis robbed her of her ability to play the piano, but her joints were so sore and stiff that even such mundane tasks as getting out of bed in the morning or rising from a chair had become laborious and painful. Her eyesight was failing and she was beginning to experience memory loss. It all must have been terribly frightening.

Despite these physical shortcomings, however, aus der Ohe fulfilled her promise to write of the golden age. This touching reminiscence of her student days, her third and final letter to Rachmaninoff, is the last we know of aus der Ohe. Beyond this there is nothing more.

 June 24, 1932, Feast of St. John

Dear Sergei Vasilych,

My dear charitable and generous Sergei Vasilych,

 Again and again you support me, always helping

me in these difficult days. A new gift from you is more than what heaven could have given me. Thank you, thank you, I thank the Lord for you.

Yes, you are so right! Looking at the piano now with great sorrow, I think about the Master and how he wanted his tradition to go on. I fulfilled this last point for he confided his art to us, and what is more: he gave his soul to all of his students. You asked me how things would have turned out for you then . . . you would have probably been the youngest, as I used to be, but we all heard of your talent as pianist and composer. You ask about the Weimarische Luft [the air (spirit) of Weimar]. Did Sasha show you the beautiful photos that we all took, informally, of the Master in this studio fashioned in the style of the Hofgärtnerei [Liszt's residence in Weimar]? I hang on to all of them in order to help my failing memory.

Yes, Sasha was right: he was the favorite, no doubt about it. The Master often looked at him pensively, thinking about his poor son, Daniel,[300] for whom he prayed every day. But of all the days that I can recall, the best one was when he [Sasha] and Hugo [Mansfeldt] played the Dante-Symphony for all of us. The Master was so flattered and so humble, he warmly embraced the cheeks and hands of the two performers as if they were his own children—we were his children. He loved the performance, and there was resounding applause. Yes, I do have the photos you mention, taken in 1884 or during my visit in 1885—I no longer remember. Yes, the close friends of my youth—Rosenthal[301] who approached everything with no fear, like a wild lion; the shy Mansfeldt,[302] who looked so unemotional, was so playful and always had a mischievous gleam in his eye and soul. Sasha,[303] with his music, looked so young. He could play anything with such ease, but he was unique in his performance of the Totentanz. Nobody dared touch this music when it was brought to ear. I even saw the Master watching, almost with envy, the way he made the piece move. Young Emil,[304] whom I still see occasionally in Berlin, played with hands of gold, brilliant as the sun, especially the Ballades and Etudes, and all Chopin. How beautiful was his cantabile. The last time he was here, I forget now when it was, he spoke about recording concertos[305] (if this could not be done, Sergei Vasilych, you could do it. The Master's continuum should not be broken. You are his grandson). Reisenauer.[306] Oh! Poor man! Did anyone worry about Reisenauer? He was such an adorable child, but he had no affinity for the Master's music—his was for Beethoven, for Schubert, both of them enormous. Of course, there was my dear Bagby; where would I be without him? He really attended to me, before and during my years in America. But that is another story.

And you ask: the Master was always satisfied with my interest in his music, though I regret this was not very easy for the public. He was happy to hear it played, but he remained discreet whenever I included it in the program. Sasha will help you to obtain it if this is of interest to you, but you may find it unusual.[307]

You say that Sasha prepared a version of the Master's Sonata for you. But I ask you to be careful— and between us, now; we loved dear Sasha immensely, as you well know, but he always thought that he could still improve what was already done and accomplished.

However, I should stop now, because this letter has taken a big part of my day and I tire easily. My heart is full of gratitude and blessings, dear Sergei Vasilych, to you and to your comforting angel in my time of trial.

Adele aus der Ohe

Aus der Ohe had written beautiful, eloquent, thoughtful letters throughout her entire life and now even this joy had become a struggle for her.

Her student Belle Mehus remembered, "there was a reserved dignity about aus der Ohe and she never discussed her private life. I did not know how old she was and she was careful never to give two dates that could be put together to determine her age. A palsy had developed in her hands and writing became difficult. Later her eyesight became poor and the last time I went to Europe while she was alive, I could not see her—I was told by Mrs. Meischner that she was no longer seeing anyone."

Many years earlier, in an interview with *Metropolitan Magazine,* aus der Ohe spoke of the philosophy that had guided her throughout her life:

One's art is like the trunk of a tree: it appears to be a single pillar and the fruit it bears is of one kind, but the roots of the tree must seek far and wide for its nourishment, pushing out new roots in all directions. The musician must likewise seek knowledge from every source to sustain and strengthen his art. I have reached the point where nothing is great, nothing is small, all life is of divine import, and we, as individuals, are all working toward the perfection of the great whole, whether we are cognizant of the fact or not. The wise know the purpose of their efforts and struggles; the foolish grope blindly.[308]

Postlude

The end came on December 8, 1937. She was seventy-six years old. The following day *The New York Times* published this obituary.

Announcement was made here last night of the death yesterday morning in Berlin of Adele aus der Ohe, one of the last surviving pupils of Franz Liszt. Born in Germany about 1865, she had been an invalid for some years, and having lost her fortune with the inflation of the mark, had been aided since April, 1928, by a pension from the Bagby Music Lover's Foundation, Inc. of this city.

Miss aus der Ohe studied music with Kullak in Berlin before beginning her work under Liszt, which lasted for seven years. Making her debut with an orchestra in Berlin, she later played throughout Europe and, beginning in 1887, toured the United States annually for seventeen consecutive years as a soloist with leading orchestras and as a concert pianist. She composed the music for several piano pieces and songs.[309]

Claudio Arrau remembered that, although he never heard Adele play, as a boy in Berlin he met her often. She and Martin Krause, his teacher who was also a Liszt student, were good friends, and Krause liked her very much. Krause took Arrau often on his visits to aus der Ohe. She was a link to the master and Krause wanted the young Arrau to absorb as much of everyone's remembrances of Liszt as possible. Arrau remembered her as a very distinguished lady. "She was one of Liszt's last pupils if not the very last and the youngest."[310]

Music In Darkness

BY RICHARD GILDER[311]

I

At the dim end of day
I heard the great musician play:
Saw her white hands now slow, now swiftly pass;
Where gleamed the polished wood, as in a glass,
The shadow hands repeating every motion.
Then did I voyage forth on music's ocean,
Visiting many a sad or joyful shore,
Where storming breakers roar,
Or singing birds made music so intense,
So intimate of happiness or sorrow,
I scarce could courage borrow
To hear those strains: well-nigh I hurried thence
To escape the intolerable weight
That on my spirit fell when sobbed the music:
late, too late, too late!
While slow withdrew the light
And, on the lyric tide, came in the night.

II

So grew the dark, enshrouding all the room
In a melodious gloom,
Her face growing viewless; line by line
That swaying form did momentarily decline
And was in a darkness lost.
Then white hands ghostly turned, tho' still they tost
From tone to tone; pauseless and sure as if in perfect light;
With blind, instinctive, most miraculous sight,
On, on they sounded in that world of night.

III

Ah, dearest one; was this thy thought, as mine,
As still the music stayed?
"So shall the loved ones fade,
Feature by feature, line on lovely line;
For all our love, alas,
From twilight into darkness shall they pass!

We in that dark shall see them nevermore,
But from our spirits they shall not be banished;
For on and on shall the sweet music pour
That was the sound of them, the loved, the vanished;
And we, who listen, shall not lose them quite
In that mysterious night."

Appendix A
Adele aus der Ohe's Published Compositions

Op. 1 Four Songs (Voice and Piano) New York, Schirmer,
1895
Text by Richard Watson Gilder
From *The New Day*
  "The Birds Were Singing"
  "A Birthday Song"
  "Not From the Whole Wide World"
  "Thistle-Down"

Op. 2 Suite (Piano Solo) New York, Schirmer, 1895
  Bourée
  Sarabande
  Menuet
  Gavotte

Op. 3 Concert Etude in C major (Piano Solo) New York,
Schirmer, 1895

Op. 4 Piano Pieces (Piano Solo) New York, Schirmer, 1897
Melody in F
Slumber Song
Rustic Dance

Op. 5 Five Songs (Voice and Piano) New York, Schirmer, 1897
Text by Richard Watson Gilder
"Rose-Dark the Solemn Sunset"
"After Sorrow's Night"
"Cradle Song"
"I Care Not if the Skies are White"
"Winds to the Silent Morn"

Op. 6 Two Songs (Voice and Piano) New York, Schirmer, 1897
Text by Adalbert von Chamisso
"The Orphans"
Text by Robert Underwood Johnson
"I Grieve To See These Tears"

Op. 7 Two Songs (Voice and Piano) New York, Schirmer, 1897
Text by Robert Underwood Johnson
"I Begged A Kiss From A Little Maid"
"Some Said They Did But Play At War"

Op. 8 Suite in E major (Piano Solo) Berlin, Ries and Erler
Prelude

Sarabande
Bourée
Air
Gavotte
Gigue

Op. 9 Four Pieces (Piano Solo) Berlin, Ries and Erler, 1901
Eine Sage (Legend)
Waltzes
Novellette
Spinnlied (Spinning Song)

Op. 10 Two Pieces (Piano Solo) New York, Schirmer, 1902
Melodie
Berecuse

Op. 11 Mazurka (Piano Solo) New York, Schirmer, 1902

Op. 12 Three Pieces (Violin and Piano) New York,
Schirmer, 1903
Mazurka
Romanze
Die Elfe tanzt (Dancing Elf)

Op. 13 Concert Etude No. 2 (Piano Solo) New York,
Schirmer, 1906
Am Springbrunnen—Eine Erinnerung an die
Villa d'Este (At the Fountain—A Remembrance
of the Villa d'Este)

Op. 14 Five Pieces (Piano Solo) New York, Schirmer, 1906
      Morgenliedchen (Morning Song)
      Pastorale
      Waltzes
      Lustiges Intermezzo (Merry Interlude)
      Am Sommerabend (On a Summer Evening)

Op. 15 (Concerto for Piano and Orchestra)

Op. 16 Violin Sonata in F-sharp major (Violin and Piano)
New York, Schirmer, 1906

Appendix B
Adele aus der Ohe's Concert Repertoire

Auber-Liszt
  Tarantella di Bravura from "La Muette"

Aus der Ohe
  Etude Op. 3
  Legend Op. 9 No. 1
  Melody Op. 4 No. 1
  Sonata in F-sharp for piano and violin Op. 16
  Spinning Song Op. 9 No. 4
  Suite No. 1 Op. 2
  Suite No. 2 Op. 8
  Valse

Bach
  Chromatic Fantasy and Fugue BWV 903
  English Suite No. 3 in G minor BWV 808
  Fantasia in C minor BWV 906

French Suite No. 5 in G major BWV 816
Italian Concerto BWV 971

Bach-Liszt
Fantasy and Fugue in G minor BWV 542

Bach-Saint-Saens
Gavotte in B minor

Bach-Tausig
Toccata and Fugue in D minor BWV 565

Beethoven
Choral Fantasy Op. 80
Concerto No. 2 in B-flat Op. 19
Concerto No. 5 in E-flat Op. 73 ("Emperor")
Sonata in C major Op. 2 No. 3
Sonata in F major Op. 10 No. 2
Sonata C-sharp minor Op. 27 No. 2 ("Moonlight")
Sonata in E-flat Op. 31 No. 3
Sonata in C major Op. 53 ("Waldstein")
Sonata in F minor Op. 57 ("Appassionata")
Variations in C minor WoO. 80

Brahms
Concerto No. 2 in B-flat Op. 83
Waltz

Chopin
Andante Spianato and Polonaise Op. 22

Ballade No. 1 in G minor Op. 23
Ballade No. 3 in A-flat Op. 47
Berceuse Op. 57
Concerto No. 1 in E minor Op. 11
Etudes Op. 25 Nos. 1, 2, 3, and 9
Various Nocturnes including:
Nocturne in B major Op. 9 No. 3
Nocturne in F-sharp major Op. 15 No. 2
Nocturne in C-sharp minor Op. 27 No. 1
Nocturne in D-flat major Op. 27 No. 2
Nocturne in F minor Op. 55 No. 1
Polonaise in A-flat Op. 53
Sonata in B-flat minor Op. 35
Various Waltzes including:
Valse in E minor
Waltz in A-flat Op. 34 No. 1
Waltz in A-flat Op. 42
Waltz in C-sharp minor Op. 64 No. 2

Chopin-Liszt
Chant Polonaise ("My Joys")

Couperin
"Le Rossingnol" in A minor ("The Nightingale")

Floersheim, Otto
Lullaby

Foote, Arthur
Prelude and Fugue in D minor Op. 15

Franck
    Sonata for Violin and Piano in A major

Gotthelf, Felix
    Piano Sonata
    "Zur Dämmerstunde" ("Twilight") (Three Fantasy
    Pieces)

Grieg
    Piano Sonata in E minor Op. 7

Huss, Henry Holden
    Concerto in B major Op. 10
    Prelude Appassionato Op. 7 No. 1

Kullak, Franz
    "Die heiligen drei Brunnen bei Trafoi"
    ("The Sacred Three Springs near Trafoi")

Liszt
    Concert Etude in D-flat ("Un sospiro")
    Concert Etude No. 1 ("Waldesrauschen")
    Concert Etude No. 2 ("Gnomenreigen")
    Concerto No. 1 in E-flat
    Concerto No. 2 in A major
    Hungarian Fantasy for Piano and Orchestra
    Hungarian Rhapsody No. 2
    Hungarian Rhapsody No. 9 ("Carnival of Pest")
    Hungarian Rhapsody No. 12
    Liebestraum No. 3 ("Love Dream")

Mephisto Waltzes Nos. 2 and 3
Nocturne No. 1
Polonaise in E major
Spanish Rhapsody
Tarantella di Bravura
Transcendental Etudes:
Eroica
Ricordanza
Etude in F minor
Valse Oubliée

Mason, William
Album Leaf in E-flat

Mendelssohn
Concerto No.1 in G minor Op. 25
Presto Op. 7 No. 7
Songs Without Words Op. 67 No. 4 ("Spinning Song")
Songs Without Words in F major Op. 85
Variations Serieuses in D minor Op. 54

Mozart
Fantasy in D minor

Mozart-Liszt
Don Juan Fantasy—from *Don Giovanni*

Paderewski
Minuet à l'antique

Poldini, E.
> Idylle Op. 23 No. 1

Raff
> Rigaudon

Rameau
> La Tambourin

Rubinstein, Anton
> Barcarolle in F minor
> Concerto No. 3 in G major Op. 45
> Concerto No. 4 in D minor Op. 70
> Valse

Scarlatti
> Capriccio
> Pastorale

Schubert
> Fantasy in C major Op. 15 ("Wanderer")
> Impromptu in F minor Op. 142 No. 1
> Impromptu in B-flat Op. 142 No. 3
> Moments Musicaux Op. 94
> Sonata in B-flat D. 960

Schubert-Liszt
> "Gretchen am Spinnrade" ("Gretchen at the Spinning Wheel")
> "Serenade"

Schumann

    Aria

    Carnaval Op. 9

    Concerto in A minor Op. 54

    Etudes Symphoniques Op. 13

    Faschingsschwank aus Wien Op. 26

    Fantasy in C major Op. 17

    Fantasiestücke Op. 12

    In der Nacht

    Fable

    Ende vom Lied

    Papillons Op. 2

    Piano Quartet in E-flat Op. 47

    Piano Quintet in E-flat Op. 44

    Sonata in G minor Op. 22

Sgambati

    Nocturne

Taubert

    Piano Concerto No. 1 Op. 18

Tausig

    Symphonic Ballade Op. 1c (*Das Geistershiff*) ("The Ghost Ship")

    Nachtfalter ("Moths")—Strauss waltz transcription

    Valse Caprice

Tchaikovsky

"Chant sans Paroles" ("Song without Words")

Concerto No. 1 B-flat minor Op. 23

Concerto No. 2 in G major Op. 44

Theme and Variations Op. 19

Vogrich, Max

Concerto in E minor

Passepied

Wagner-Liszt

"Isoldes Liebestod" ("Isolde's Love-Death") from *Tristan and Isolde*

"Spinning Song" from *The Flying Dutchman*

Weber

Koncertstücke for Piano and Orchestra Op. 79

Zarebski

Grand Polonaise in F-sharp Op. 6

Endnotes

1. Albert Morris Bagby, "Some Pupils of Liszt." *The Century Illustrated Monthly Magazine*, March 1888.
2. The correct capitalization is Adele aus der Ohe (lowercase *a* in aus), similar to *v* in Ludwig van Beethoven. This is how aus der Ohe always signed her name and it is the convention I have adhered to in this book, despite the fact that nearly all American publications print her name as Adele Aus der Ohe. I capitalize Aus der Ohe only when her last name begins a sentence; adhering, of course, to standard English rules of starting a sentence with a capital letter.
3. Nearly all biographical literature gives December 11, 1864 as aus der Ohe's birthdate, which is incorrect. Church baptismal records from Hanover provide the correct date of February 11, 1861.
4. A literal translation of the name aus der Ohe is "from the Heights." The family originated in Hanover and the Ohe was a pasture region near Hanover. In the *Hanover Chronicle: From the Beginnings to the Present; Numbers, Dates, Facts*, we read that in 1682, 207 head of cattle were kept by the citizens in the Ohe. By 1730, parts of the Ohe were leased out since only around fifty head of cattle were still herded there. In 1843, sixteen garden communities were consolidated into two municipalities: Glocksee (with Ohe) and Hanover. Then in 1869, the Prussian home secretary approved the annexation of the suburb of Glocksee and the Ohe by the provincial capital of Hanover, and the modern city of Hanover was born.
5. This is not a typographical error. The baptismal records indicate Adelheid, ending in a *d*, but for Adele the spelling is Adelheit.
6. S. J. Barrows, "A Great Musician at Home," *The Criterion Magazine*, April 1901.
7. Amy Fay, *Music-Study in Germany in the Nineteenth Century*. New York: Dover Publications, 1965.

8. This formal certificate, on letterhead and complete with a wax seal, is housed in the archives of the Staatsbibliothek in Berlin, and was made available for our perusal by the kind and helpful staff of that great institution.

9. Max Eliot, June 1887; Samuel E. Asbury, *Letters, portraits and criticism concerning the concert pianist Adele Aus der Ohe.* College Station, Texas, 1951.

10. Karl Pohlig (1864-1928) was a German pianist and conductor. He led the Philadelphia Orchestra from 1907 to 1912.

11. Carl Lachmund, *Living with Liszt From the Diary of Carl Lachmund, an American Pupil of Franz Liszt, 1882–1884.* Stuyvesant, New York: Pendragon Press, 1995.

12. *Das Geisterschiff*, Symphonic Ballade Op. 1c (The Ghost Ship) is about eight minutes of incredibly difficult and demanding music.

13. Louis Coonen was a French pianist.

14. Weimar, *The Musical World.* September 1877.

15. The Goethe and Schiller Archive in Weimar kindly made available this draft of Liszt's letter to aus der Ohe.

16. Translation note: There are a couple of minor uncertainties: The word "indess" probably should have been crossed out, since it is an incomplete word and is followed by a capitalized "Wenn," which has to be the beginning of a sentence. At the end of the sentence after "Adele aus der Ohe" there seem to be a couple of words missing to make sense of everything. This could well be due to the fact that these were just thoughts scribbled down, so there are indeed mistakes. Perhaps what Liszt intended was something like: "If you want to tell . . . Mrs. Jachmann-Wagner that it is recommended that she look on Adele aus der Ohe with favor as an accomplished pianist, I would be completely in agreement with that."

17. Foreign Correspondance, "Music in Berlin," *The Monthly Musical Record*, February 1883.

18. Carl Lachmund, *Living with Liszt From the Diary of Carl Lachmund, an American Pupil of Franz Liszt, 1882–1884.* Stuyvesant, New York: Pendragon Press, 1995.

19. Foreign Correspondance, "Music in Berlin," *The Monthly Musical Record*, December 1883.

20. Albert Morris Bagby, "Some Pupils of Liszt." *The Century Illustrated Monthly Magazine,* March 1888.

21. Hans Bronsart von Schellendorff (1830–1913) and his wife Ingeborg (1840–1913) were prominent musicians in Hanover and both were students of Liszt. Liszt dedicated his Second Piano Concerto to Hans Bronsart who played the premiere performance of it in Weimar. Ingeborg Bronsart was a composer as well as a touring concert pianist.

22. Hans von Bulow (1830–1894) was one of Liszt's most famous students and one of the great musicians of the nineteenth century. His wife was Liszt's daughter, Cosima.

23. Bagby is in error here. Adele was actually eight when the family moved to Berlin.

24. Liszt's actual letter: "Esteemed Fellow Artist, You have succeeded excellently with the preludes. They offer to the piano-playing world a desirable

help. With thanks and pleasure the dedication is accepted by Franz Liszt."
S. J. Barrows, "A Great Musician at Home." *The Criterion Magazine*, April 1901.

25. August Göllerich, *The Piano Master Classes of Franz Liszt, 1884–1886*. Bloomington, Indiana: Indiana University Press, 1996.

26. Ibid.

27. Ibid.

28. Samuel E. Asbury, *Letters, portraits and criticism concerning the concert pianist Adele Aus der Ohe*. College Station, Texas, 1951.

29. *New York Times*, December 24, 1886.

30. *New York Mail and Express*, December 24, 1886. http://www.archive. org/stream/inmemoriumoooaklrich/inmemoriumoooaklrich_djvu.txt (accessed April 2011).

31. *New York World*, December 24, 1886. http://www.archive.org/stream/inmem oriumoooaklrich/inmemoriumoooaklrich_djvu.txt (accessed April 2011).

32. *New York Evening Post*, December 24, 1886. http://www.archive.org/stream/ inmemoriumoooaklrich/inmemoriumoooaklrich_djvu.txt (accessed April 2011).

33. *New York Sun*, December 24, 1886. http://www.archive.org/stream/inmem oriumoooaklrich/inmemoriumoooaklrich_djvu.txt (accessed April 2011).

34. *New York Critic*, January 7, 1887. http://www.archive.org/stream/inmemo riumoooaklrich/inmemoriumoooaklrich_djvu.txt (accessed April 2011).

35. *New York Tribune*, December 24, 1886. http://www.archive.org/stream/ inmemoriumoooaklrich/inmemoriumoooaklrich_djvu.txt (accessed April 2011).

36. *New York Commercial Advertiser*, December 24, 1886. http://www.archive. org/stream/inmemoriumoooaklrich/inmemoriumoooaklrich_djvu.txt (accessed April 2011).

37. *New York Star*, December 24, 1886. http://www.archive.org/stream/inmem oriumoooaklrich/inmemoriumoooaklrich_djvu.txt (accessed April 2011).

38. *New York Musical Courier*, December 29, 1886. http://www.archive.org/ stream/inmemoriumoooaklrich/inmemoriumoooaklrich_djvu.txt (accessed April 2011).

39. Henry Edward Krehbiel, "Review of the New York Musical Season 1886-1887," *BiblioBazaar* 2008, and Henry Edward Krehbiel, "Review of the New York Musical Season 1887-1888," *BiblioBazaar* 2008.

40. *New York Mail*, January 8, 1887. http://www.archive.org/stream/inmemori umoooaklrich/inmemoriumoooaklrich_djvu.txt (accessed April 2011).

41. *New York Herald*, http://www.archive.org/stream/inmemoriumoooaklrich/ inmemoriumoooaklrich_djvu.txt (accessed April 2011).

42. *New York Tribune*, http://www.archive.org/stream/inmemoriumoooaklrich/ inmemoriumoooaklrich_djvu.txt (accessed April 2011).

43. Ibid.

44. *New York Times*, March 15, 1887.

45. *New York Critic*, http://www.archive.org/stream/inmemoriumoooaklrich/ inmemoriumoooaklrich_djvu.txt (accessed April 2011).

46. *Evening Transcript*, Monday, March 28, 1887; Samuel E. Asbury, *Letters, portraits and criticism concerning the concert pianist Adele Aus der Ohe*. College Station, Texas, 1951.

47. *Boston Courier*, March 27, 1887. http://www.archive.org/stream/inmemo riumoooaklrich/inmemoriumoooaklrich_djvu.txt (accessed April 2011).

48. *Musical Matters*, June 1887; Samuel E. Asbury, *Letters, portraits and criticism concerning the concert pianist Adele Aus der Ohe*. College Station, Texas, 1951.

49. *Boston Daily Advertiser*, http://www.archive.org/stream/inmemorium oooaklrich/inmemoriumoooaklrich_djvu.txt (accessed April 2011).

50. Max Eliot was the pen name of Mrs. Granville Alden Ellis, an American author, critic, and journalist.

51. Max Eliot, June 1887; Samuel E. Asbury, *Letters, portraits and criticism concerning the concert pianist Adele Aus der Ohe*. College Station, Texas, 1951.

52. Howard Malcom Ticknor (1836–1905) was one of the leading music critics in Boston.

53. Howard Malcom Ticknor; Samuel E. Asbury, *Letters, portraits and criticism concerning the concert pianist Adele Aus der Ohe*. College Station, Texas, 1951.

54. Letter from Adele aus der Ohe to Mr. Dennis, May 14, 1887.

55. This is high praise. Adelina Patti (1843–1919) was one of the most famous singers in operatic history. She was renowned for her beautiful tone and splendid technique.

56. *New York World*, http://www.archive.org/stream/inmemoriumoooaklrich/ inmemoriumoooaklrich_djvu.txt (accessed April 2011).

57. *New York Times*, http://www.archive.org/stream/inmemoriumoooaklrich/ inmemoriumoooaklrich_djvu.txt (accessed April 2011).

58. *New York Sun*, http://www.archive.org/stream/inmemoriumoooaklrich/ inmemoriumoooaklrich_djvu.txt (accessed April 2011).

59. *New York Star*, http://www.archive.org/stream/inmemoriumoooaklrich/ inmemoriumoooaklrich_djvu.txt (accessed April 2011).

60. Letter from Adele aus der Ohe to Mrs. Gilder, July 13, 1887.

61. Ibid., May 23, 1890.

62. Ibid., August 6, 1888.

63. The Gilder archives are housed in the Lilly Library at Indiana University, where one precious folder contains over fifty letters from Adele aus der Ohe to Mrs. Gilder. They are a treasure, providing so much insight not only into the life of the great pianist, but also attesting to a long and lovely friendship. The first letter is dated January 7, 1887, and the last October 9, 1911—a friendship of twenty-five years.

64. A dazzling panoply of names! Ignace Paderewski (1860–1941), the most famous pianist of his generation; Helena Modjeska (1840–1909), the most famous Shakespearian actress of her generation; Eleonora Duse (1858–1924), another hugely famous actress; Joseph Jefferson (1829–1905), one of the most famous American comedians of the nineteenth century and also famous for his portrayal of Rip Van Winkle; Rudyard Kipling (1865–1936), one of the most famous authors of his generation; John Singer Sargent

(1856–1925), the leading portrait painter of his generation; Cecilia Beaux (1855–1942), another famous portrait painter.

65. William Webster Ellsworth, *A Golden Age of Authors*. Boston: Houghton Mifflin Company, 1919.
66. http://docsouth.unc.edu/fpn/harrison/harrison.html (accessed July 2011).
67. *New York Musical Courier*, November 23, 1887. http://www.archive.org/stream/inmemoriumoooaklrich/inmemoriumoooaklrich_djvu.txt (accessed April 2011).
68. *New York Sun*, January 10, 1888. http://www.archive.org/stream/inmemoriumoooaklrich/inmemoriumoooaklrich_djvu.txt (accessed April 2011).
69. *The World*, January 10, 1888. http://www.archive.org/stream/inmemoriumoooaklrich/inmemoriumoooaklrich_djvu.txt (accessed April 2011).
70. *New York Herald*, January 10, 1888. http://www.archive.org/stream/inmemoriumoooaklrich/inmemoriumoooaklrich_djvu.txt (accessed April 2011).
71. *Boston Herald*, http://www.archive.org/stream/inmemoriumoooaklrich/inmemoriumoooaklrich_djvu.txt (accessed April 2011).
72. *New York Sun*, March 1888. http://www.archive.org/stream/inmemoriumoooaklrich/inmemoriumoooaklrich_djvu.txt (accessed April 2011).
73. *The World March*, 1888. http://www.archive.org/stream/inmemoriumoooaklrich/inmemoriumoooaklrich_djvu.txt (accessed April 2011).
74. *Philadelphia Times*, http://www.archive.org/stream/inmemoriumoooaklrich/inmemoriumoooaklrich_djvu.txt (accessed April 2011).
75. *Philadelphia Evening Bulletin*, http://www.archive.org/stream/inmemoriumoooaklrich/inmemoriumoooaklrich_djvu.txt (accessed April 2011).
76. *Chicago Morning News*, http://www.archive.org/stream/inmemoriumoooaklrich/inmemoriumoooaklrich_djvu.txt (accessed April 2011).
77. Programme Toccata and Fugue—Bach-Tausig Sonata in C-sharp minor Op. 27—Beethoven Pastorale and Capriccio—Scarlatti Aria—Schumann Menuet a l'antique—Paderewski Spinning Song—Mendelssohn Andante Spianato et Polonaise—Chopin Rhapsodie Hongroise No. 9—Liszt.
78. Sappho was one of the greatest lyric poets of ancient Greece while Rhadamanthos was, according to legend, made judge of the underworld. The imagery is that Sappho recites heavenly poetry accompanied by her harp while Rhadamanthos scratches out punishments for the damned with a goose quill pen.
79. This is a rather humorous statement. Pactolus was a river in ancient Lydia (modern day Turkey) that was famous for the gold that washed up with the sand. The imagery is of a region in America that, while remote, is very pleasant.
80. "The Aus der Ohe Concert," *Oberlin Review*, June 12, 1888.
81. Letter from Adele aus der Ohe to Mrs. Gilder, October 16, 1888.
82. Leroy Ostransky, *Perspectives on Music*. New Jersey: Prentice Hall, 1963.
83. Alan Walker, *Franz Liszt, Volume 1: The Virtuoso Years 1811–1847*. New York: Cornell University Press, 1983.
84. *New York Sun*, January 5, 1889. http://www.archive.org/stream/inmemoriumoooaklrich/inmemoriumoooaklrich_djvu.txt (accessed April 2011).

85. *Werner's Magazine*, January 1897.
86. Cornelia Dyas, "Moriz Rosenthal and Adele aus der Ohe," *Metropolitan Magazine*, January 1899.
87. *St. Paul Daily Globe*, January 18, 1889.
88. Letter from Adele aus der Ohe to Mrs. Gilder, April 8, 1889.
89. Ibid., June 17, 1889.
90. *New York Sun*, November 1889. http://www.archive.org/stream/inmemor iumoooaklrich/inmemoriumoooaklrich_djvu.txt (accessed April 2011).
91. *The Beacon*, Boston, December 28, 1889. http://www.archive.org/stream/ inmemoriumoooaklrich/inmemoriumoooaklrich_djvu.txt (accessed April 2011).
92. *The Evening Transcript*, Boston, December 28, 1889. http://www.archive. org/stream/inmemoriumoooaklrich/inmemoriumoooaklrich_djvu.txt (accessed April 2011).
93. *The Sunday Herald*, Boston, December 29, 1889. http://www.archive. org/stream/inmemoriumoooaklrich/inmemoriumoooaklrich_djvu.txt (accessed April 2011).
94. *The Boston Daily Traveler*, December 1889. http://www.archive.org/stream/ inmemoriumoooaklrich/inmemoriumoooaklrich_djvu.txt (accessed April 2011).
95. *The Boston Daily Advertiser*, December 1889. http://www.archive.org/ stream/inmemoriumoooaklrich/inmemoriumoooaklrich_djvu.txt (accessed April 2011).
96. *The Boston Times*, February 10, 1889. http://www.archive.org/stream/ inmemoriumoooaklrich/inmemoriumoooaklrich_djvu.txt (accessed April 2011).
97. Letter from Adele aus der Ohe to Mrs. Gilder, December 14, 1889.
98. *Pittsburgh Dispatch*, February 14, 1890.
99. The program: (Notice that numbers 2, 4, and 6 in the program are songs. She shared the program with a tenor, Mr. Charles Steven, according to the custom of the time.)
    1. Beethoven—Sonata in E-flat Op. 31 No. 3
    2. Denza—"Song of the Nubian Girl"
    3. Scarlatti—Pastorale and Capriccio
    4. Paderewski—Minuet a'l'antique
    5. Raff—Rigaudon
    6. MacDowell—Two Songs
    7. Chopin—Valse in A-flat Op. 34, Berceuse, Ballade in G minor, Andante Spianato et Grande Polonaise
    8. Meyer-Helmund—"Youth"
    9. Liszt—Tarantelle di Bravura
100. *The Chronicle*, University of Michigan, March 1, 1890.
101. Program: (A contralto, Miss Mary Buckley, provided the customary even-numbered vocal selections)
    1. Beethoven—Sonata in C major Op. 53 *"Waldstein"*
    2. Bizet—"Adieux de L'Hotesse Arabe"

3. Bach—Gavotte in D minor
4. Chopin—Nocturne in B major Op. 9 No. 3 and Valse in A-flat Op. 42
5. Waldham—"Come to Me"
6. Schubert—Fantasie in C major Op. 15 *"Wanderer"*
7. Grieg—"Autumnal Gale"
8. Liszt—Nocturne and Don Juan Fantasie

102. Program (at last without vocal interruptions!):
    1. Beethoven—Sonata in F minor Op. 57 "Appassionata"
    2. Kullak—The Sacred Three Springs at Trafoi
    3. Aus der Ohe—Suite No. 2 in E major Op. 8 (new)
    4. Mendelssohn—Two Songs Without Words
    5. Chopin—Nocturne in C-sharp minor Op. 27, Four Etudes Op. 25 Nos. 1, 2, 3, 9 and Valse in E minor
    6. Liszt—Concert Etude in D-flat and Hungarian Rhapsody No. 12

103. Program:
    1. Bach—Fantasy in C minor
    2. Schubert—Impromptu in F minor Op. 142 No. 4
    3. Beethoven—Variations in C minor
    4. Chopin—Sonata in B-flat minor Op. 35
    5. Schumann—Three Fantasy Pieces from Op. 12
       In der Nacht, Fabel, Ende vom Lied
    6. Aus der Ohe—Eine Sage (Legend) and Etude
    7. Liszt—Nocturne and Tarantelle di Bravura

104. *Chicago Daily Tribune*, March 1890.
105. Letter from Adele aus der Ohe to Mrs. Gilder, March 15, 1890.
106. *The Morning Call*, San Francisco, November 19, 1890.
107. Ibid.
108. Ibid., November 21, 1890.
109. Ibid., November 26, 1890.
110. Ibid., November 30, 1890.
111. Ibid., November 21, 1890.
112. *Los Angeles Times*, December 11, 1890.
113. Harold Schonberg, *The Great Conductors*. New York: Simon and Schuster, 1967.
114. *New York Times*, March 18, 1896.
115. Letter from Adele aus der Ohe to Mrs. Gilder, June 17, 1889.
116. Ibid., June 27, 1889.
117. Ibid., May 23, 1890.
118. Elkhonon Yoffe, *Tchaikovsky in America*. New York: Oxford Press, 1986.
119. *Los Angeles Times*, February 3, 1893.
120. *Los Angeles Times*, October 1, 1899.
121. *Polish Music Journal*, Vol. 5, No. 2, Winter 2002. http://www.usc.edu/dept/polish_music/PMJ/issue/5.2.02/trointroduction.html (accessed July 2011).
122. Richard Watson Gilder, *The Poems of Richard Watson Gilder*. Boston: Houghton Mifflin Company, 1908.
123. *New York Times*, January 13, 1906.

124. Modeste Tchaikovsky. Translated and Edited by Rosa Newmarch. *The Life and Letters of Peter Ilyich Tchaikovsky*. New York: John Lane Company, 1914.

125. Elkhonon Yoffe, *Tchaikovsky in America*. New York: Oxford Press, 1986.

126. *New York Times*, May 10, 1891.

127. Reprinted with permission.

128. http://oldwgms.bonnint.net/bigbookwritings_knabe.shtm (accessed April 2011).

129. Elkhonon Yoffe, *Tchaikovsky in America*. New York: Oxford Press, 1986.

130. Ibid.

131. Samuel E. Asbury, *Letters, portraits and criticism concerning the concert pianist Adele Aus der Ohe*. College Station, Texas, 1951.

132. Letter from Tchaikovsky to William von Sachs, November 15/27, 1892.

133. An original poster advertising the concert is kindly provided by Brett Langston of the Tchaikovsky Research Project.

134. Charles Gounod had died only about a week earlier at the age of seventy-five.

135. *Chicago Daily Tribune*, February 25, 1894.

136. *Music Trade Review*, New York, 1906. http://www.arcade-museum.com/mtr/MTR-1906-42-22/index.php?page_no=03&frame=MTR-1906-42-22-03.pdf (accessed July 2011).

137. Letter from Adele aus der Ohe to Mrs. Gilder, February 3, 1893.

138. The Program (surprisingly devoid of bravura)
    1. Beethoven—Sonata in F major Op. 10 No. 2
    2. Schumann—Papillons Op. 2
    3. Ries—"Trennung"
       (Miss Katherine Gordon, voice)
    4. Tchaikovsky—Chant sans Paroles
    5. Schubert—Moment Musical
    6. Schubert-Liszt—Serenade
    7. Chopin-Liszt—Chant Polonais
    8. Chopin—Nocturne in F-sharp and Etude
    9. Tausig—Valse-Caprice
    10. Massenet—"Beaux yeux que j'aime"
    11. Vidal—"Printemps Nouveau"
        (Miss Katherine Gordon, voice)
    12. Liszt—Hungarian Rhapsody No. 12

139. *St. Paul Daily Globe*, February 26, 1893.

140. Letter from Adele aus der Ohe to Mrs. Gilder, May 15, 1893.

141. Letter from Adele aus der Ohe to Whilhem Gericke, January 22, 1894.

142. http://en.wikipedia.org/wiki/4-4-0 (accessed April 2011).

143. Ibid.

144. Letter from Adele aus der Ohe to Mrs. Gilder, October 1904.

145. *St. Paul Globe*, August 7, 1904.

146. Ibid., January 29, 1904.

147. A listing of all known repertoire performed by Adele aus der Ohe is included in Appendix B.

148. *The Minneapolis Journal*, January 9, 1904.

149. Samuel E. Asbury, *Letters, portraits and criticism concerning the concert pianist Adele Aus der Ohe*. College Station, Texas, 1951. Philip Hale, February 17, 1897.

150. Ibid., February 28, 1899.

151. Comparisons between Venus and Diana were typically used to show dual aspects of femininity. Venus was the Roman goddess of love and beauty and personified the sensuous and sexual side of femininity. (A cestus was a belt worn by women in ancient Greece). Diana was the Roman goddess of purity and virginity. She personifies the heavenly world and is indifferent to the baser world of the flesh.

152. Samuel E. Asbury, *Letters, portraits and criticism concerning the concert pianist Adele Aus der Ohe*. College Station, Texas, 1951. R.R.G., November 16, 1904.

153. Ibid., February 9, 1897.

154. Ibid., February 15, 1899.

155. *London Times*, February 15, 1902.

156. *St. Paul Globe*, January 29, 1904.

157. *Chicago Daily Tribune*, February 25, 1894.

158. S. J. Barrows, "A Great Musician at Home," *The Criterion Magazine*, April 1901.

159. Ibid.

160. There is a recording of it on the Hyperion label by Howard Shelley and the Tasmanian Symphony Orchestra.

161. This concerto has never been recorded. There is a score in the Harvard Library which is also available online. I have seen the score and it is, in a word, "gnarly." Perhaps one of you ambitious readers will be inspired to make the premiere recording!

162. Samuel E. Asbury, *Letters, portraits and criticism concerning the concert pianist Adele Aus der Ohe*. College Station, Texas, 1951. February 9, 1889.

163. Ibid.

164. Ian Hobson has recorded it on Hyperion Records with the BBC Scottish Symphony Orchestra, Martyn Brabbins conducting.

165. Samuel E. Asbury, *Letters, portraits and criticism concerning the concert pianist Adele Aus der Ohe*. College Station, Texas, 1951. November 13, 1903.

166. August Göllerich, *"The Piano Master Classes of Franz Liszt, 1884–1886."* Bloomington, Indiana: Indiana University Press, 1996.

167. Emma Eames (1865–1952) was one of the great opera singers of the late nineteenth and early twentieth centuries.

168. Samuel E. Asbury, *Letters, portraits and criticism concerning the concert pianist Adele Aus der Ohe*. College Station, Texas, 1951. January 16, 1897.

169. *Music Trade Review*, New York, 1900. http://www.arcade-museum.com/mtr/ MTR-1900-31-25/index.php?page_no=09&frame=MTR-1900-31-25-09. pdfpdf (accessed July 2011).

170. Foreign Correspondance, "Music in Berlin," *The Monthly Musical Record*, February 1883.

171. Letter from Adele aus der Ohe to Mr. Dennis, May 14, 1887.

172. *New York Times*, December 14, 1904.

173. Letter from Adele aus der Ohe to Mrs. Gilder, October 24, 1897.

174. Ibid., April 20, 1898.

175. Ibid., November 17, 1901.
176. Ibid., July 13, 1905.
177. Ibid., January 4, 1909.
178. Ibid., April 20, 1898.
179. Rupert Hughes, "Women Composers," *The Century Magazine*, March 1898.
180. Ibid.
181. Ibid.
182. Ibid.
183. Ibid.
184. Adelbert von Chamisso (1781–1838) was a German poet and botanist.
185. Rupert Hughes, "Women Composers," *The Century Magazine*, March 1898.
186. Ibid.
187. Robert Underwood Johnson (1853–1937) was an American writer and became editor of *The Century Magazine* upon the death of Richard Gilder.
188. Rupert Hughes, "Women Composers," *The Century Magazine*, March 1898.
189. Ibid.
190. Ibid.
191. *New York Times*, November 23, 1898.
192. *Musical America*, New York, November 26, 1898.
193. *The Commercial Advertiser*, New York, November 23, 1898.
194. *New York Sun*, November 23, 1898.
195. *Music Trade Review*, New York, 1904. http://www.arcade-museum.com/mtr/ MTR-1904-39-6/index.php?page_no=09&frame=MTR-1904-39-6-09. pdf (accessed July 2011).
196. *New York Times*, October 16, 1904.
197. *Boston Globe*, January 3, 1905.
198. *New York Times*, January 10, 1905.
199. *New York Times*, March 3, 1893.
200. *The Morning Call*, San Francisco, March 12, 1893.
201. S. J. Barrows, "A Great Musician at Home," *The Criterion Magazine*, April 1901.
202. Letter from Adele aus der Ohe to Mrs. Gilder, October 24, 1897.
203. *London Times*, June 19, 1897.
204. Letter from Adele aus der Ohe to Mrs. Gilder, April 20, 1898.
205. *New York Times*, March 29, 1898.
206. Ibid., April 3, 1898.
207. Letter from Adele aus der Ohe to Mrs. Seidl, April 2, 1898.
208. *New York Times*, September 22, 1898.
209. *Music Trade Review*, New York, 1897. http://www.arcade-museum.com/mtr/ MTR-1897-24-18/index.php?page_no=09&frame=MTR-1897-24-18-09. pdf (accessed July 2011).
210. Letter from Adele aus der Ohe to Mrs. Gilder, November 12, 1895.
211. *New York Daily Tribune*, November 7, 1898.
212. Letter from Adele aus der Ohe to Mrs. Gilder, September 13, 1903.
213. Ibid., August 16, 1905.
214. Samuel E. Asbury, *Letters, portraits and criticism concerning the concert pianist Adele Aus der Ohe*. College Station, Texas, 1951. February 11, 1899.

215. Samuel E. Asbury, *Letters, portraits and criticism concerning the concert pianist Adele Aus der Ohe*. College Station, Texas, 1951. February 28, 1899.

216. Letter from Mathilde aus der Ohe to Mr. Barrows, undated.

217. *Music Trade Review*, New York, 1900. http://www.arcade-museum.com/mtr/ MTR-1900-31-22/index.php?page_no=08&frame=MTR-1900-31-22-08. pdf (accessed July 2011).

218. Letter from Mathilde aus der Ohe to Mr. Barrows, September 26, 1900.

219. Letter from Adele aus der Ohe to Mrs. Gilder, August 16, 1905.

220. *New York Times*, March 24, 1901.

221. Letter from Adele aus der Ohe to Mrs. Gilder, May 14, 1901.

222. Ibid., November 17, 1901.

223. *The Morning Post*, London. December 6, 1901.

224. *The Era*, London, December 7, 1901.

225. Letter from Adele aus der Ohe to Mrs. Gilder, December 14, 1901.

226. *Fort Worth Weekly Gazette*, October 26, 1890.

227. Letter from Adele aus der Ohe to Mrs. Gilder, April 23, 1904.

228. *Music Trade Review*, New York, 1904. http://www.arcade-museum.com/mtr/ MTR-1904-39-20/index.php?page_no=13&frame=MTR-1904-39-20-13. pdf (accessed July 2011).

229. W. L. Hubbard, *Chicago Daily Tribune*, November 23, 1903.

230. Samuel E. Asbury, *Letters, portraits and criticism concerning the concert pianist Adele Aus der Ohe*. College Station, Texas, 1951, November 16, 1904.

231. *Music Trade Review*, New York, 1903. http://www.arcade-museum.com/mtr/ MTR-1903-37-23/index.php?page_no=21&frame=MTR-1903-37-23-21. pdf (accessed July 2011).

232. Ibid., 1901. http://www.arcade-museum.com/mtr/MTR-1901-32-9/ index.php?page_no=05&frame=MTR-1901-32-9-05.pdf (accessed July 2011).

233. Ibid., 1903. http://www.arcade-museum.com/mtr/MTR-1903-37-22/index .php?page_no=13&frame=MTR-1903-37-22-13.pdf (accessed July 2011).

234. Letter from Adele aus der Ohe to Mrs. Gilder, April 23, 1904.

235. *Music Trade Review*, New York, 1904. http://www.arcade-museum.com/mtr/ MTR-1904-38-19/index.php?page_no=04&frame=MTR-1904-38-19-04. pdf (accessed July 2011).

236. *New York Times*, January 13, 1906.

237. *Boston Daily Globe*, January 21, 1906.

238. M. A. DeWolff Howe. *The Boston Symphony Orchestra a Historical Sketch*. Boston: Houghton Mifflin Company, 1914.

239. Peekskill is about forty miles north of New York City, in Westchester County, and is situated on the east side of the Hudson River. Lake Mohegan is nearby.

240. *New York Times*, August 21, 1906.

241. Ibid., August 29, 1906.

242. Born Countess of Münster.

243. Translator's note: From "Zum Andenken der Fürstin Anna-Amalia" (In memory of the Duchess Anna Amalia) by Johann Wolfgang von Goethe after

the death of Duchess Anna Amalia of Brunswick-Wolfenbuttle on April 10, 1807.

244. Lawrence Gilman Edward MacDowell, *A study* (New York: John Lane Company, 1908).

245. Ibid.

246. Ibid.

247. Letter from Adele aus der Ohe to Mrs. Gilder, January 4, 1909.

248. Harriet Brower, *Piano Mastery.* New York: Frederick A. Stokes Company, 1915.

249. www.lyceumclub.org/en/history.htm#s1 (accessed September 1, 2011).

250. Ibid.

251. Harriet Brower, *Piano Mastery.* New York: Frederick A. Stokes Company, 1915.

252. Letter from Adele aus der Ohe to Mrs. Beach, September 27, 1911.

253. Letter from Adele aus der Ohe to Mrs. Gilder, October 9, 1911.

254. Belinda L. Davis, *Home Fires Burning.* North Carolina: The University of North Carolina Press, 2000.

255. William Menkel, "Living Conditions in Germany and Austria." *The American Review of Reviews,* February 1917.

256. Kriegsbrot was a poor quality bread made partially with potates due to the shortage of flour. It was tasteless and soggy and the Germans hated it.

257. William Menkel, "Living Conditions In Germany and Austria." *The American Review of Reviews,* February 1917.

258. Letter from Adele aus der Ohe to Professor Rich. Sternke, July 1920.

259. Ibid., to August Weiss, June 1910.

260. Robert Underwood Johnson, *The Winter Hour And Other Poems.* New York: The Century Co., 1892.

261. Letter from Adele aus der Ohe to Robert Johnson, February 9, 1893.

262. *New York Times*, January 4, 1927.

263. In 2003, Dover Publications combined and published these three books in one volume. A shocking example of just how forgotten aus der Ohe has become is revealed by the fact that in the process of combining the three volumes, Dover excluded several interviews, including aus der Ohe's. We therefore know of her interview only from the original 1915 publication.

264. Harriet Brower, *Piano Mastery.* New York: Frederick A. Stokes Company, 1915.

265. Alma Mehus Studness (1902–2001) spoke very lovingly of her time with aus der Ohe during an interview conducted in the mid-1980s at her home in Devil's Lake, North Dakota.

266. Letter from Adele aus der Ohe to Miss Mehus, June 26, 1924.

267. Ibid., October 26, 1923.

268. Ibid., letter undated.

269. Fergusson, Adam. *When Money Dies.* London: William Kimber & Co. Ltd., 1975.

270. Friedrich, Otto. *Before the Deluge: A Portrait of Berlin in the 1920s*: New York: Harper & Row, 1972.

271. Fergusson, Adam. *When Money Dies.* London: William Kimber & Co. Ltd, 1975.

272. Ibid.

273. Ibid.

274. Friedrich, Otto. *Before the Deluge: A Portrait of Berlin in the 1920s.* New York: Harper & Row, 1972.

275. Fergusson, Adam. *When Money Dies.* London: William Kimber & Co. Ltd., 1975.

276. This sounds almost preposterous, but there is an actual photograph of this as it is occurring on page 224 of Belinda Davis' book, *Home Fires Burning.*

277. Fergusson, Adam. *When Money Dies.* London: William Kimber & Co. Ltd., 1975.

278. Letter from Adele aus der Ohe to Miss Mehus, October 26, 1923.

279. Adam Smith, *Paper Money.* New York: Dell Publishing Co., 1981.

280. Larry Allen, *Encyclopedia of Money.* New York: Checkmark Books, 2001.

281. Otto Friedrich, *Before the Deluge: A Portrait of Berlin in the 1920s.* New York: Harper & Row, 1972.

282. Rentenmark translates literally as Debt Security Mark. It served as an interim currency to stabilize the German economy and was valid until 1948.

283. Adam Smith, *Paper Money.* New York: Dell Publishing Co., 1981.

284. Matthew Josephson, *Life among the Surrealists, a memoir.* New York: Holt, Rinehart and Winston, 1962.

285. Letter from Adele aus der Ohe to Alma Mehus, December 13, 1928.

286. Ibid., October 5, 1930.

287. Ibid., 1924.

288. Ibid., 1927.

289. Otto Friedrich, *Before the Deluge: A Portrait of Berlin in the 1920s.* New York: Harper & Row, 1972.

290. Ibid.

291. Ibid.

292. Ibid.

293. Letter from Adele aus der Ohe to Alma Mehus, December 13, 1928.

294. Hyman Rovinsky was a young pianist in America in the 1920s.

295. *New York Times,* December 6, 1925.

296. Minnie Hauk (1851–1929) was a noted opera singer.

297. *New York Times,* February 24, 1929.

298. The first edition of Rachmaninoff's concertos was ornately decorated.

299. This is a Russian music publishing house located in Berlin that Rachmaninoff used for his European business transactions.

300. Liszt's only son Daniel (1839–1859) died at the age of twenty from tuberculosis. It was a dreadful blow to Liszt.

301. Moriz Rosenthal (1862–1946) was Polish. He first studied with Liszt from 1876 to 1878 and then from 1884 to 1886.

302. Hugo Mansfeldt (1844–1932) was German born but moved to the United States at the age of fifteen. He studied with Liszt from 1884–1886.

303. Alexander Siloti (1863–1945) was Russian and studied with Liszt from 1883 to 1886.

304. Emil von Sauer (1862–1942) was German and studied with Liszt from 1884 to 1886.
305. This recording project did actually become a reality. In December 1938, at the advanced age of seventy-six, von Sauer recorded both Liszt concertos.
306. Alfred Reisenauer (1863–1907) began his studies with Liszt about 1874 and continued until 1886. He unfortunately became an alcoholic and died at the age of forty-four.
307. It is difficult to understand what aus der Ohe is saying in this paragraph. It is true that already during Liszt's lifetime his music began to fall out of favor with the public and pianists who programmed Liszt did so at the risk of incurring criticism. Liszt was aware of this. Perhaps that is what she is alluding to. The final sentence is simply a mystery. Is she telling Rachmaninoff that Sasha (Siloti) can help him to find Liszt's style of playing but that Rachmaninoff might find Liszt's style of playing unusual? Or is she simply referring to the repertoire and suggesting that Sasha can help Rachmaninoff explore Liszt's compositions but that he might find them unusual?
308. Cornelia Dyas, "Moritz Rosenthal and Adele aus der Ohe." *Metropolitan Magazine*, January 1899.
309. *New York Times,* December 9, 1937.
310. Letter from Friede Rothe to LaWayne Leno, September 20, 1982.
311. Richard Watson Gilder, *The Poems of Richard Watson Gilder.* Boston: Houghton Mifflin Company, 1908.

Bibliography

http://www.klassika.info/Komponisten/Adele/index.html

http://mugi.hfmt-hamburg.de/A_lexartikel/lexartikel.
php?id=ausd1864

Allen, Larry. *Encyclopedia of Money*. New York: Checkmark
Books, 2001.

Asbury, Samuel E. *Letters, portraits and criticism concerning
the concert pianist Adele Aus der Ohe*. College Station,
Texas, 1951.

Bagby, Albert Morris. *Liszt's Weimar*. New York: A. S.
Barnes and Company, 1961.

_____. "Some Pupils of Liszt," *The Century Illustrated
Monthly Magazine* No. XXXV, 1887.

_____. "A Summer with Liszt in Weimar," *The Century
Illustrated Monthly Magazine*, No. XXXII, 1886.

Barrows, S. J. "A Great Musician at Home," *The Criterion Magazine*, April 1901.

Berger, Ernst. *Franz Liszt: A Chronicle of His Life in Pictures and Documents*. Princeton, New Jersey: Princeton University Press, 1989.

Brower, Harriet. *Piano Mastery*. New York: Frederick A. Stokes Company, 1915.

Davis, Belinda J. *Home Fires Burning: Food, Politics, and Everyday Life in World War 1 Berlin*. Chapel Hill, North Carolina: The University of North Carolina Press, 2000.

Dyas, Cornelia. "Moriz Rosenthal and Adele aus der Ohe," *The Metropolitan Magazine*, January 1899.

Ehrlich, A. *Celebrated Pianists of the Past and Present*. Philadelphia: Theodore Presser, 1894.

Ellsworth, William Webster. *A Golden Age of Authors*. Boston: Houghton Mifflin Company, 1919.

Fay, Amy. *Music Study in Germany in the Nineteenth Century*. New York: Dover Publications, 1965.

Fergusson, Adam. *When Money Dies*. London: William Kimber & Co. Ltd., 1975.

Friedrich, Otto. *Before the Deluge: A Portrait of Berlin in the 1920s*. New York: Harper & Row, 1972.

Gilder, Richard Watson. *The Poems of Richard Watson Gilder*. Boston: Houghton Mifflin Company, 1908.

Gilman, Lawrence. *Edward MacDowell: A study.* New York: John Lane Company, 1908.

Göllerich, August. *The Piano Master Classes of Franz Liszt, 1884–1886.* Bloomington, Indiana: Indiana University Press, 1996.

Howe, M. A. DeWolff. *The Boston Symphony Orchestra: a Historical Sketch.* Boston: Houghton Mifflin Company, 1914.

Hughes, Rupert. "Women Composers." *The Century Illustrated Monthly Magazine,* No. LV, March 1898.

Jenkins, Walter. *The Remarkable Mrs. Beach, American Composer.* Warren, Michigan: Harmonie Park Press, 1994.

Johnson, Robert Underwood. *The Winter Hour and Other Poems.* New York: The Century Company, 1892.

Josephson, Matthew. *Life among the Surrealists, a memoir.* New York: Holt, Rinehart and Winston, 1962.

Krehbiel, Henry Edward. *Review of the New York Musical Season 1886–1887.* New York, Novello, Ewer & Co., 1887.

_____. *Review of the New York Musical Season 1887–1888.* New York, Novello, Ewer & Co., 1888.

Lachmund, Carl. *Living with Liszt from the Diary of Carl Lachmund, an American Pupil of Franz Liszt, 1882–1884.* Stuyvesant, New York: Pendragon Press, 1995.

Menkel, William. "Living Conditions in Germany and Austria." *The American Review of Reviews*, January–June 1917.

Mlynek, Klaus and Waldemar R. Röhrbein, Ed. assisted by Dieter Brosius. *Hanover Chronicle: From the Beginnings to the Present; Numbers. Dates. Facts*. Hanover: Schlütersche, 1991.

Ostransky, Leroy. *Perspectives on Music*. Englewood Cliffs, New Jersey: Prentice Hall, 1963.

Schonberg, Harold. *The Great Pianists*. New York: Simon and Schuster, 1963.

_____. *The Great Conductors*. New York: Simon and Schuster, 1967.

Smith, Adam. *Paper Money*. New York: Dell Publishing Co., 1981.

Swafford, Jan. *Johannes Brahms: A Biography*. New York: Alfred A. Knopf, 1998.

Tchaikovsky, Modeste. Translated and Edited by Rosa Newmarch. *The Life & Letters of Peter Ilyich Tchaikovsky*. New York: John Lane Company, 1914.

The Monthly Musical Record. March 1883.

The Oberlin Review. Volume 15, 1887.

Thomas, Theodore and George Upton. *Theodore Thomas: A Musical Autobiography*. Chicago: A.C. McClurg & Co., 1905.

Walker, Alan. *Franz Liszt, Volume 1: The Virtuoso Years 1811–1847*. Ithaca, New York: Cornell University Press, 1983.

_____. *Franz Liszt, Volume 2: The Weimar Years 1848–1861*. Ithaca, New York: Cornell University Press, 1989.

_____. *Franz Liszt, Volume 3: The Final Years 1861–1886*. New York: Alfred A. Knopf, 1996.

Yoffe, Elkhonon. *Tchaikovsky in America: The Composer's Visit in 1891*. New York: Oxford University Press, 1986.

About the Author

LaWayne Leno was born and raised in rural North Dakota where he studied piano with Belle Mehus and her sister, Alma Mehus-Studness. He continued his piano studies with Oxana Yablonskaya of the Juilliard School, and completed his education at the University of Mary in Bismarck, North Dakota. He became a certified public accountant and, after a twenty-year career in computer consulting, returned to his first love—piano teaching. LaWayne currently resides in Dellwood, Minnesota.